CONFLICT OF CONVICTION,

A Reappraisal of Quaker Involvement in the American Revolution

William C. Kashatus III

UNIVERSITY
PRESS OF
AMERICA

Lanham • New York • London

Copyright © 1990 by

University Press of America®, Inc.
4720 Boston Way
Lanham, Maryland 20706

3 Henrietta Street
London WC2E 8LU England

Library of Congress Cataloging-in-Publication Data

Kashatus, William C., 1959-
Conflict of conviction : a reappraisal of Quaker involvement
in the American Revolution / William C. Kashatus III.
p.   cm.
1. United States—History—Revolution, 1775-1783—Quakers.
2. Quakers—United States—History—18th century.
3. Society of Friends—United States—History—18th century.
4. United States—History—Revolution, 1775-1783—Religious aspects.
I. Title.
E269.F8K37   1990   973.3'089286—dc20   90–39160 CIP

ISBN 0–8191–7882–9 (alk. paper)
ISBN 0–8191–7883–7 (pbk.: alk. paper)

 The paper used in this publication meets the minimum requirements of
American National Standard for Information Sciences—Permanence
of Paper for Printed Library Materials, ANSI Z39.48–1984.

For my mother, who gave me my faith and for my father, who taught me to respect that of God in each person, regardless of their station in life

.   .   .   my love for them is eternal.

Contents

Foreword

At the time of the American Revolution, Quakerism with its strong pacifist testimony was one of the leading religious persuasions in the American colonies. The religious, social, and political ideals of the Society of Friends, especially as exemplified in the colony of Pennsylvania, played a significant role in the thinking of the time.

Already by the middle of the eighteenth century, Pennsylvania Quakers had gone from rags to riches, from the poverty of the settlement years to the affluence produced by the rich land of the colony on the one hand, and the opportunities of imperial trade on the other. Thus the world was exerting a strong pull on the spiritual domain of the meeting house, and provoked among young and old alike a conflict of conviction as to whether or not to participate in the Revolutionary movement. William Kashatus' chapter on the Valley Forge community underscores this pattern of events as well as the diverse response of Friends to the cause of American independence, a result of their conflict of conviction.

Despite their religious rearing many Friends were carried into the actual conflict, often thus impelled by their interpretation of their inherited idealism. The author demonstrates that such revolutionary leaders as Thomas Paine and General Nathanael

Greene, as well as the founders of the Free Quaker Society, were influenced in their thinking and way of life by their Quaker education. The most significant contribution in this collection of essays, however, is Kashatus' reappraisal of the Free Quaker movement.

The term "Free Quaker" evokes for many the image of a group of people who betrayed one of the cardinal testimonies of historical Quakerism. For others it evokes the concept of people who had the courage to stand for their conviction as to the right action under the leading of the Inner Light. This difference of opinion is illustrative of the conflict between individual leading and group guidance which has historically presented disciplinary problems for the Society of Friends.

Little extensive research has been done on the Free Quakers in the two centuries since their emergence. The only account of their history was published at the end of the last century by Charles Wetherill, a descendent of the founder of the Free Quaker movement, Samuel Wetherill, Jr. Kashatus' chapter on the Free Quakers breaks new ground by re-examining not only their emergence, but also by investigating the basic motives of those who participated in the movement. The author has been aided in his thoughtful analysis by the appearence of the letters of Samuel Wetherill, Jr., which were recently acquired by the Friends Historical Library of Swarthmore College.

The Society of Friends viewed the failure of many Quakers to maintain the peace testimony as indicated in the Discipline, and outlined in subsequent official statements, as a rejection of true Quakerism. The author clearly demonstrates, however, that many of those who became Free Quakers held strong religious convictions as basic to their action, and that they believed their convictions were soundly based on early Quaker history.

It is interesting to note that, in some aspects, notably the absence of a disciplinary provision for disownment, the practice

of the Free Quakers foreshadows that of the present day Society of Friends.

Arthur J. Mekeel, author
The Relation of the Quakers
to the American Revolution
(1979)

Introduction

Since Arthur J. Mekeel published The Relation of the Quakers to the American Revolution in 1979, most of the research that has been completed on Friends in the Revolutionary era has emphasized their adherence to pacifism or the Society's attempt to reform its membership to honor that principle. These studies have reinforced the popular misconception that all Quakers, historically, have been absolutely against war and participation in civil government during a time of war, their identifying feature being the Peace Testimony. Even among Friends themselves there is a great misunderstanding of the complexity of the issues involved in the Peace Testimony, many having elevated that principle to an almost universally accepted creed. This collection of essays attempts to address that misconception by bringing a new understanding of the diversity and complexity of the Quaker involvement in the American Revolution and by shedding new light on the personal, theological and moral dilemmas -- as well as sacrifices -- many Friends experienced in their decision to comply with the war effort.

The first essay, on Tom Paine and the ideology of the American Revolution, examines the intellectual contribution to the Revolution made by a founding father who was genuinely Quaker in his personal convictions. The depth of Paine's commitment to Quakerism as well as his adaptation of those values to the Whig principles of the time period are reflected in "Common Sense," the pamphlet that mobilized popular support for the American Revolution. Nathanael Greene's contribution to the War for Independence, the topic of the second essay, was more militant in nature and more personally devastating than Paine's. Caught between his devotion to Quaker principles and strong feelings of patriotism, the Rhode Island Friend emerges as a tragic hero. By going to war, Greene paid the price of membership in the Society for a violation of his own internalized values. His recurrence to Quakerism, in his personal associations and form of worship, along with a resurgent self-doubt over the righteousness of his participation in the war serve as testimony to the spiritual crisis the New England Quaker suffered throughout the Revolution. Greene's experience was, indeed, a conflict of conviction. While these two essays address the personal involvements of individual Quakers in the Revolution, the third and fourth essays deal with the social and spiritual dynamics of two Quaker communities as they confront the challenges to their life styles brought on by the war.

The Quaker community of Valley Forge, Pennsylvania, had a mixed reception to the American Revolution since there was a broad spectrum of compliance and non-compliance with the war effort among its members. This diversity of response can be attributed to the permissiveness in matters of religious discipline that evolved among Pennsylvania Friends nearly a half century before the Revolution itself. By 1777, when the Continental Army set up a winter encampment in their environs, the distinctions between "patriot" and "Quaker" had become sufficiently blurred for the Valley Friends and, in some cases, those terms were even synonymous. The experience of this Quaker community reinforces the complexity of the Friends' involvement in the Revolution. Finally, the fourth essay reappraises the motivation of the Free Quakers in establishing a religious body independent of the Society of Friends. This group, which has long been considered a band of social deviants by many historians, genuinely believed their compliance with the war effort to be consistent with the Lamb's War ethic of the early Quakers. By following the example of the first Friends, the Free Quakers gave testimony to the righteousness of the American Revolution.

Most of the essays in this collection were first published as brief articles in 1984, 1986 and 1987 in Quaker History and The Valley Forge Historical Journal. But through the counselling of others, I became convinced that a more comprehensive treatment of Quakers who were involved in the American Revolution was needed. The topic of this study was first suggested to me by Hugh Barbour of Earlham College and was nurtured by Professors William G. McLoughlin, Donald M. Scott and Gordon S. Wood during my work on a master's degree at Brown University. The fruition of this project, however, could not have taken place without the constant guidance of Arthur J. Mekeel, former editor of Quaker History, and Michael Zuckerman of the University of Pennsylvania. Both encouraged my efforts along the way, reading and re-reading the various drafts of the manuscript and offering their constructive counsel.

Special thanks are due to the staff members of the Quaker Collection at Haverford College, the Friends Historical Library at Swarthmore College, the Manuscript Department at the Historical Society of Pennsylvania, the Rhode Island Historical Society and the Newport Historical Society for their ready assistance. Research was made possible through grants provided by the History divisions of Independence National Historical Park, Valley Forge National Historical Park and the Episcopal Academy.

When one works on a project for nearly a decade, a number of personal debts also accumulate. Mine begin with my parents, Balbina and William, and my students at the Riverdale Country School, Abington Friends School and the Episcopal Academy. Their enthusiasm for learning, their example of giving their best effort and the warmth of their spirits challenged me to strive for excellence as a teacher and writer. Hugh Barbour, Peter Cline and Randall Shrock, my mentors at Earlham College, cultivated a passion for history in me and encouraged me to continue that passion in graduate school. I am also grateful to Helen and Richard Femino, my surrogate parents in Rhode Island, who were responsible for keeping me at Brown during some rather trying times and for enhancing my interest in their native New England. During the years that I have worked on this project I benefitted greatly from discussing my ideas with Sarah and Charles Northrop, the best friends a person could have, and Joan and David Dutcher, chief historians with the National Park Service. Their forthright criticism and advice has manifested itself in the numerous revisions of my work.

Above all, I am indebted to my wife, Jackie. Although she is a scientist by profession, she understands the historian's unyielding desire for a monastic lifestyle when he is engaged in research. Without her patience, support and love, my dream of writing a book would never have come true.

Philadelphia, Pa.
August 1989

Chapter I

Thomas Paine & the Ideology of the American Revolution

The publication of Thomas Paine's "Common Sense" in January, 1776, mobilized public support for the principles of the American Revolution. Paine's pamphlet clearly articulated the already existing, but latent, values of the republican ideology in American society: the sacrifice of individual interests to the greater good of the whole, an ambivalent combination of equality of opportunity and equality of condition, a distrust for power and the necessity to control it and a conviction of the natural and inalienable rights of men. [1]

The immediate influence of this republican ideology on the thought of American revolutionaries has been attributed to the writings of the Commonwealthmen. [2] However, the identification of the Protestant Dissenting tradition, among the broader influences of the ideology, has encouraged some historians to suggest that Quaker thought played a crucial role in the formation of American ideals. [3] Effective proof of such an assertion has remained elusive however, since any direct impact on the political climate of 1776 Philadelphia appears to be negated by the Society of Friends' opposition to involvement in political affairs and its uncompromising stance on pacifism. [4] Moreover, an ideological connection can be indicated if a founding father were proven to be sincerely Quaker in his thought, but, to date, none has been identified. [5] In this respect, the socio-religious thought of Thomas Paine has been overlooked as evidence of a Quaker influence on the ideology of the American Revolution.

Although his Quaker upbringing is an established fact, the problem of Paine's Quakerism, with regard to its impact on the ideology of the American Revolution, is a very complex one. [6] The identification of such an influence is difficult to prove not only because most of Paine's correspondence and autobiographical materials, providing insight for his thought, were accidently destroyed by fire over a century ago, [7] but also in order to depict Paine in his entirety requires a knowledge of Revolutionary America, England and France as well as a familiarity with eighteenth century science, theology and political thought. Accordingly, the current purpose is not to negate those other strands of thought by proposing an exclusively Quaker influence on Paine's ideology, but rather to suggest that Quaker thought -- and not the Deism that influenced his writing in later years -- was the predominant strain of influence on Paine's ideology during his first years in America.

Quakerism, which arose in England during the religious upheaval of the Cromwellian period in the middle of the 17th century was based on the fundamental doctrine of that of God in every man or the "inner light." This conviction maintains that the "relation between Christ and man is an organic one." Accordingly, all human beings are "aware of their common relation to one God and, hence, to each other." [8] This religious concept, combined with a pragmatic stress on the ethical principles recorded in the Scriptures, produced a strong sense of social responsibility among the Quakers. This social and ethical consciousness resulted in three distinct social testimonies which became distinguishing marks of the early Quaker movement as well as of the Society of Friends subsequently.

The most prominent of these testimonies is the Peace testimony, announced as early as 1660. The early Quakers believed that through an appeal to the Inner Light in all men the pride and vanity and greed which were the cause of war would be eliminated. Consequently, the Friends refused both the payment of war taxes and conscription into the militia. This strong adherence to pacifism was unique among all other seventeenth and eighteenth century non-conformist sects, earning the Quakers, at various times, either the silent respect or the condemnation of the ruling government. [9]

The second testimony, that of equality, was founded on the premise that every human being, regardless of race, sex or religion, possesses the same Inner Light, thus making all persons equal in the eyes of God. This conviction manifested itself in the equal role of women in the ministry and subsequently in the anti-slavery activities of the Friends as well as in their support of women's involvement in social reform. Consequently, the Society of Friends became a pioneer in the abolition of slavery and in the struggle for women's rights.

Finally, the Quaker testimony on simplicity involved a direct witness to the world against self-love and vanity. Simplicity was illustrated by the adoption of plain dress, the use of the plain language and the utilitarian education which young Friends received.

These socio-religious convictions were expressed in the Quakerism of the generations of both Thomas Paine and his father, although the respective environments of these two Quaker generations were distinctly different. Paine's father, Joseph, grew up under the last vestiges of the early evangelizing Quaker movement, which still bore marks of the prophetic fervor of the first generation. [10] Thomas, however, was a product of the subsequent quietist period, an era marked by increasing withdrawal from society at large. During this time, Quakers became less active in their outward ministry while cultivating their inward spiritual endowments. [11]

Although the quietist period has frequently been considered responsible for the passiveness of the Society at that time, quietism did not spell lethargy and inaction; rather it was a revised emphasis on the right way to initiate action. In fact, the quietist period, with the decline of an evangelizing ministry, was a time of much inner spiritual activity which ultimately enabled the Friends to disregard accepted social ideas and prompted their activity as pioneers in various social causes. This fact is significant in an examination of the Quaker influence on young Thomas Paine.

The Quaker milieu which surrounded Paine during the period 1737-1777 commenced with the influence of his father and his birthplace. Paine was born in the village of Thetford in the county of Norfolk, England, on January 29, 1737. His Quaker upbringing resulted from his father's strong religious convictions which assured a religiously-guarded education for the young Paine who later wrote:

> My father being of the Quaker profession, it was my good fortune to have an exceedingly good moral education, and a tolerable stock of useful learning. Though I went to the grammar school, I did not learn Latin, not only because I had no inclination to learn languages, but because of the objection the Quakers have against the books in which the language is taught. I had some talent for poetry; but this I rather repressed than encouraged as leading too much into the field of imagination. [12]

This religiously-guarded education was illustrative of the quietist period's attempt to shield Quaker children in their education from the worldly influences of imaginative writings and the classical languages. [13] Similarly, according to quietist practice Paine was taken "to the meetinghouse in Thetford from the age of six where he spent at least eight hours each week." [14] This practice of protracted worship resulted from the quietist emphasis on the need constantly to cultivate the "immediate connection of the human soul with God." [15]

However, Joseph Paine, a product of the earlier evangelizing period, made certain that quietism was not the only aspect of Quakerism which influenced his son. He made every attempt to instill the spirit of martyrs in his son's blood by maintaining a collection of prophetic tracts and Journals detailing the personal religious experiences of these first Quaker missionaries and martyrs. [16] Such a library, which "formed in multitudes of Quaker homes, the main body of reading matter," provided a susceptible Quaker youth like Tom with "the formative ideas of his faith." [17] Also Joseph Paine's indefatigable spirit of social responsibility influenced "his son's rejection of hierarchies in church and state and his active support for reforms ranging from anti-slavery to the abolition of dueling." [18]

Moreover, a penchant for dissent was fostered in both Joseph and his son by their surrounding environment. The Quaker historian, William Braithwaite, maintains that Norfolk, the county in which Paine was reared, was a hot-bed of the Quaker dissenting tradition. By 1699 Quaker dissent had become so rampant in the county that its Justice and Grand Jurors drafted a petition to the House of Commons requesting that steps be taken to suppress the sect. The petition was apparently unsuccessful, since "Norfolk became a very strong center of Quaker life in the early 1700's." [19]

The next formative period of Paine's life came when he moved to Lewes in the county of Sussex. There his Quaker milieu expanded. This period of Paine's life, 1768-1774, is critical for an understanding of his political convictions since it was in Lewes that he came to adopt the political and social consciousness which would manifest itself later in his actions during his first years in America. More important, Paine adopted these political convictions through his company with *middle-class* and *working-class* Quakers, not the more affluent intellectuals who espoused deism.

Paine arrived in the village of Lewes in 1768 as an exciseman and established a residence at the Bull House. The Bull House was the village's social center consisting of lodgings, a tobacco shop, a meetinghouse and, most significantly, the White Hart Inn, the "resort of Lewes' intellectual circle." [20] Here Paine's Quakerism became tempered by the prevailing Whig political convictions of the time. To be sure, Paine mixed with those of various religious professions, but his more intimate acquaintances were from the Quaker milieu surrounding him during his first forty years, 1737-1777.

Paine lived in the quarters of the Quaker Samuel Ollive, the tobacconist at Bull House, who was a member of the White Hart intellectual circle. [21] His closest companion, however, was the Quaker Thomas "Clio" Rickman, a member of Sussex Friends Meeting. [22] Together with Paine, Rickman contributed some of the most "obstinate and agitating" works to the White Hart's "Headstrong Book," a collection of prose and political essays reflecting the convictions of the Whig tradition. [23] Accordingly, Rickman maintained that "in politics Paine was at this time a Whig." [24] It would thus seem that Paine's exposure to the Whiggism of the White Hart club grounded him firmly in the ideology of that tradition.

By this time a more radical strain, the Commonwealth tradition, with roots in the age of the Puritan ascendency in England, had achieved increasing popularity. [25] The Commonwealth ideology was based on a conviction in "extending the rights of Englishmen to all mankind," freedom of thought, religious toleration and the classical form of a republican government under the English theory of a mixed constitution. [26] This ideology had been embraced by Harrington and Sidney, Locke and Newton, Hutcheson and the Scottish school and, finally, during the reign of George III, by Pownall and Wilkes. [27] Gordon Wood regards this ideology, and particularly the contributing ideas of Milton and Sidney, as the dominant intellectual influence of the American Revolution. [28] Paine's intimate contact with these influences helped to merge Quaker conviction and Whig principle in his personal ideology.

During the two year period 1772-1774 most of Paine's time was spent traveling between Sussex and London. He had volunteered to act as a lobbyist for his fellow excisemen who had become "disgruntled about their low wages and the risking of their lives for an unpopular cause." [29] At this time Paine wrote his first public appeal, "The Case of the Officers of Excise," which produced little effect as evidenced by Parliament's decision to ignore the excisemen's requests. [30] In addition, Paine's exposure to London's labor and hunger riots, [31] his witnessing of the Wilkes controversy and its rallying of the social orders behind the Commonwealth ideology, [32] and his compassion for the poor had resulted in his espousal of the Commonwealth ideology. [33] This socio-political ideology complemented and strengthened Paine's existing Quaker disregard for privilege and aristocracy and can be viewed as an inheritance of traditional Quaker political values.

The political values espoused by Quakers were best expressed in the political theory of William Penn. Penn came to support the Whig ideology actively during the years 1676-1682 when he lived in the tiny hamlet of Worminghurst, Sussex, not far from what would become Paine's residence in the town of Lewes. [34] In the elections of 1679, Penn "worked actively on behalf of Algernon Sidney," one of the founding fathers of the Commonwealth ideology. [35] In fact, Frederick Tolles maintains that Sidney's influence on Penn branded the Quaker as "a Whig and a Dissenter" who "laid down the basic Whig principles upon which Pennsylvania was founded." [36]

Penn gathered a substantial portion of the "First Purchasers" of the Pennsylvania colony from the county of Sussex where he had launched an extensive sales and advertisement campaign. [37] Many of these Quaker neighbors were familiar with Penn's political tracts, "England's Great Interest in the Choice of this New Parliament" and "One Project for the Good of England." Both treatises were written in 1679 and reflected the ardent Whig principles which the Pennsylvania proprietor implemented in his own colony. The Whig conviction of religious toleration, ably expressed in these works, was extremely attractive to the Quaker inhabitants of Sussex, and in particular to Friends in Lewes who suffered "much religious persecution" during the 1670s and 1680s. [38]

Essentially then, Penn's Holy Experiment was derived from the combination of Quaker religious thought and Whig political ideals, both of which found agreement in religious toleration and a conviction in the personal liberty exercised for the public good. Furthermore, the influence of Penn's writings, his Holy Experiment and the peaceful coexistence of a Whig-Quaker tradition permeated the subsequent generation of Sussexmen, leaving an indelible mark on Thomas Paine who, "for some years, collected taxes in that county while keeping a residence in Lewes." [39]

In short, Thomas Paine left England for the American colonies with an ideology that was grounded in Quakerism, and it was from this idealistic basis that the author of "Common Sense" adopted the complementary philosophy of Commonwealth Whiggism. This fundamental Quaker influence would also condition the milieu in which Paine moved upon arriving in Philadelphia in 1774 and was to manifest itself in his first series of socio-political writings in that American city.

Paine's strong support for the cause of American independence earned him the label "Quaker apostate." No less significant is the fact that in his friendships he consciously

8

gravitated towards those who, like himself, had been nurtured in the principles of Quakerism, not Deism. During his early years in Philadelphia, 1774-1777, Paine's Quaker milieu consisted of those Friends who had adopted the principle "that offensive war was never to be considered, but that a war of defense was Christian and therefore justifiable." [40]   Many Friends who held this opinion and whose actions contravened the Peace Testimony were disowned during the Revolutionary War. [41]

A number of these former members united in 1781 with other like-minded individuals to establish a new body known as the Free Quaker Monthly Meeting of Philadelphia. They adopted the name "since they based their rules of conduct and action on freedom from the restraints which characterized the main body of the Society." [42]   While the Free Quakers resembled the main body in their acceptance of its "general doctrines, organization and mode of conduct in worship," they differed in their "ommission of any theological statement of belief, the abolition of all offenses for disownment" and in their "encouragement to participate in civil affairs and in the military defense of the country." [43]   At the height of the Free Quaker movement in the 1790's, there were well over one hundred members, about half of whom had been disowned for participation in the war. [44]

Although Paine never officially joined the Free Quakers, he was very much in sympathy with their principles as reflected by his many intimates in that group. Had he been living in Philadelphia in 1781 and afterward he would doubtless have become an active member of the Religious Society of Free Quakers. [45]   Still, there is evidence of a "Free Quaker milieu" in Paine's American life as early as 1775 when "the company that would converse with him included patriotic Quakers such as Christopher Marshall who circulated about the city promoting independence along with Timothy Matlack, a former Quaker and brewer. [46]

Marshall, a former druggist, although disowned earlier for involvement in forgery, maintained his Quaker contacts and often attended meeting. He took an active part on the Whig side in the contest with the mother country and was elected to the Committee of One Hundred in November 1774 as well as to the Pennsylvania Provincial Council in June 1776. [47]   Matlack, like Paine, was raised in a staunch Quaker household and experienced the same religiously-guarded education. Several years later his devotion to the main tenets of Quakerism prompted him to "make a religious journey to New England in 1783" to visit the Free Quaker group in that area. [48]   At the time of his initial acquaintance with Paine, in 1775, Matlack was employed as a clerk to the Secretary of the Continental Congress. [49]   Two years later he was appointed Secretary to the Pennsylvania Assembly. In this capacity Matlack conducted a frequent correspondence with Paine, primarily discussing official business of the Assembly, and occasionally sharing personal grievances over the Society of Friends' pacifist stance in the Revolution. [50]

The most intimate companion of Paine's like-minded milieu, however, was General Nathanael Greene. In July 1776, when he volunteered as a soldier for the Continental cause, Paine requested the position of aide-de-camp to Greene at Fort Lee in Manhattan. [51]   During their brief nine month association Paine and Greene "became good friends on both political and personal grounds." [52]

Greene's religiously-guarded education in Warwick, Rhode Island, made him familiar with the most prominent Quaker texts, including Robert Barclay's *Apology* and the *Complete Works of William Penn*. [53]   Consequently Greene's socio-political ideas were "little more than a paraphrasing of old shibboleths with a good seasoning of Quaker doctrine." [54]   This fact is reflected in his inherent conflict of conviction over participation in war when, in later years, Greene declared:

> To me war was ever a business of necessity
> . . . and unavoidable from the plans of our

creation; but I am averse to it from its being
opposite to my temper and feelings.
I thought the cause of liberty was in danger,
and as it was attacked by a military force it
was necessary to cultivate a military spirit
among the people. [55]

Accordingly, the "Fighting Quaker's" annoyance with the
Friends' failure to uphold the cause of independence compelled
him to accuse the Society of hypocrisy and, subsequently, to
request that he be "put from under the care of Friends for the
future." [56]

Paine shared Greene's convictions and, if anything, this
friendship made the radical Paine more militantly patriotic and
even stronger in his condemnation of the "Tory" Quakers.
Sentiments of this kind are clearly demonstrated in the first
pamphlets of his American Crisis series, written during the nine
month association with Greene.

Paine's fervent patriotism is evidenced in the "American
Crisis #1," written in December 1776 to rally the recently
defeated army of Washington. In memorable words which have
etched themselves on countless patriotic minds throughout
American history Paine began his work:

These are the times that try men's souls.
The summer soldier and the sunshine patriot
will, in this crisis, shrink from the service of
their country; but he that stands it now,
deserves the love and thanks of man and
woman. Tyranny, like hell, is not easily
conquered; yet we have this consolation with
us that the harder the conflict, the more
glorious the triumph. What we obtain too
cheap, we esteem too lightly; it is dearness
only that gives everything its value. Heaven
knows how to put a proper price upon its
goods; and it would be strange indeed if so
celestial an article as FREEDOM should not be
highly rated. [57]

11

Subsequently, in "American Crisis #3," written in April 1777, Paine condemns the "treasonable Quakers" for their "supposed neutrality" in the Revolution. [58] His basic support of Quaker principles, however, is illustrated by the distinction Paine makes between his patriotic Quaker milieu and the Crown partisans of the Society when he states: "A religious Quaker is a valuable character and a political Quaker a real Jesuit." [59] This distinction is a significant one since it reinforces the fact that Paine's personal sympathies still rested with the religious principles of the Society. However, he had reconciled those principles with his republican convictions and thereby came to the conclusion that the truest expression of Quakerism was exhibited by those who eventually became Free Quakers. Moreover, it was this "true expression" of Quakerism that was reflected in Paine's political works during his first two years in America, writings which initiated the American Revolution by articulating the ideology of that cause for American independence.

The Quaker Influence on the Socio-political Writings of Paine, 1774-76

Thomas Paine's socio-political ideology, like that of his contemporaries, was influenced by the broad context of the European Enlightenment. This intellectual renaissance, characterized by the thought of Locke, Montesquieu, Hume and Newton, permeated the social environments of both eighteenth century England and America, leaving an indelible mark on the pamphleteers of the period. Accordingly, there are those historians who insist that Paine's first political writings, and in particular "Common Sense," mirror his later deistical works, "Rights of Man" and "Age of Reason," writings which unmistakably reflect the rationalism of the Enlightenment period. [60]

Still, when making this attempt to link the Tom Paine of 1774-76 with deism, it is important to recognize that the English radical "knew little of the writings" of the Enlightenment thinkers. [61] Nor was he "under any deistical influence during [his editorship] of the *Pennsylvania Magazine.*" [62] These facts negate any direct rationalist influence on the Thomas Paine of 1774-76, enhancing the potential influence of those with whom he did associate during this period who consisted largely of what might be called a Free Quaker milieu. In short, those characteristics that are most distinctive in Paine's writings can be attributed to Quakerism and not Deism.

Paine's first writings, as well shall see, mirror a uniquely Quaker configuration in his thought. No other writer of the period emphasizes equality, simplicity and pacifism as strongly as does Paine, or employs that specific configuration with such consistency. Paine's first writings, as editor of the *Pennsylvania Magazine* are illustrative of his Quaker influence and, more significantly, form the basis for his subsequent work "Common

Sense," the vehicle which mobilized the American public for the Revolution.

The first article Paine published entitled "African Slavery" (1774), clearly reflected a Quaker bias. The only previous statements of this type had been written by John Woolman in 1754 and Anthony Benezet in 1767, pleading respectively for the abolition of slavery and of the slave trade. [63] The impelling principle of the anti-slavery cause on the part of the Quakers was their belief in "that of God in every man." This cause had been increasingly nurtured by the Society of Friends for nearly a century in both America and England before the appearance of Paine's article in 1774. [64]

Consequently, in this first article, Paine entreats his reader to consider the argument set forth by many Friends at this time:

> With what consistency, or decency do
> Americans complain so loudly of attempts to
> enslave them, while they hold so many
> hundred thousands in slavery; and annually
> enslave many thousands more without any
> pretence of authority or claim upon them? [65]

Also consistent with his Quaker heritage is Paine's admonition: "How just, how suitable our crime is to the punishment with which Providence threatens us?" David Brion Davis in his work, *The Problem of Slavery in the Age of Revolution*, maintains that "the Quakers, more than any other religious group, had long expressed misgivings over the sinfulness of slavery, and consequently, "interpreted each step toward a total disengagement from slaveholdeing as a tangible sign of growing religious purity." [66] This fact is demonstrated by the minute of Philadelphia Yearly Meeting in adopting an anti-slavery stance in 1758:

> This meeting very earnestly and affectionately
> intreats Friends to consider seriously the
> present circumstances of these and the

> adjacent provinces, which, by the permission
> of Divine Providence, have been visited with
> the desolating calamities of war and
> bloodshed, so that many of our fellow
> [colonists] are now suffering in captivity and
> fervently desires, that . . . we may manifest
> an humbling sense of their judgements, and .
> . . would steadily observe the injunction of
> our Lord and Master to "do unto others as we
> would they should do unto us"; which it
> now appears to this meeting, would induce
> such Friends who have any slaves to set them
> at liberty. [67]

Similarly, Paine, like many Quakers of the late eighteenth century, proposed a program of gradual emancipation for blacks. Unlike the Quakers, he simultaneously advocated immediate emanicipation from monarchy. These themes formed the basis of the revolutionary's 1775 article, "A Serious Thought", which resembles the Yearly Meeting minutes of 1758, particularly in its reference to divine punishment:

> When I reflect on . . . the use [Britain]
> hath made of the discovery of this new world
> -- that the little paltry dignity of earthly kings
> hath been set up in preference to the great
> cause of the King of Kings . . . [and] that
> ever since the discovery of America she hath
> employed herself in the most horrid of all
> traffics, that of human flesh . . . hath
> yearly ravaged the hapless shores of Africa,
> robbing dominions in the west -- when I
> reflect on these, I hesitate not for a moment to
> believe that the Almighty will finally separate
> America from Britain . . . And when the
> Almighty shall have blest us, and made us a
> people dependent only upon Him, then may
> our first gratitude to be shown by an act of
> continental legislation which shall put a stop
> to the importation of Negroes for sale, soften
> the hard fate of those already here, and, in
> time, procur their freedom. [68]

Clearly, Paine's intention to equate the cause of anti-slavery with that of American independence was a true expression of his uniquely Quaker humanitarianism. Those American intellectuals who espoused deism addressed the issue with much less certainty. At best, anti-slavery was a contested issue among American whigs and, hence, cannot be considered part of the ideology adopted by the deists of the period.

Another strong connection exists between Paine's Quakerism and his position on non- violence. Paine's brief article on "Dueling," written May 1775, indicates the influence of Quaker pacifism on his thought. In this he states that the custom of duelling is a "gothic and absurd manner of accommodating cerain kinds of personal differences and of redressing . . injuries." [69] Duelling, being based on the matter of pride, is "absurd" for Paine just as it was for the Quakers who, in adherence to their Peace Testimony, sought to remove the pride and vanity which provided all cause for war. He ends his condemnation by maintaining that duelling "offers a plain illustration of how little mankind are, in reality, influenced by the principles of the religion by which they profess to be guided." [70] Again, we see the incompatibility of Quaker and Deistic thought. While Paine the Quaker displays a disdain for pride, few republican revolutionaries, particularly those from the South, would have had any principled objection to pride, rather most would have a positive affinity for it.

As much as Paine "abhorred the method of violence," his pacifism was a conditional one. [71] In July 1775, in his article "Thoughts on Defensive War" Paine acknowledges that the idealism of the Society's Peace Testimony cannot be practiced in the real world:

> I am thus far a Quaker, that I would gladly
> agree with all the world to lay aside the use of
> arms, and settle matters by negotiation; but
> unless the whole will, the matter ends and I

take up my musket and thank heaven he has
put it in my power. [72]

Still, Paine's adherence to defensive warfare is conditioned by his love of religious liberty, a truly Quaker conviction. For Paine, "political liberty (secured through the defense of property) is the visible pass which guards the religions." Therefore, he is "fully convinced that spiritual freedom is the root of political liberty." [73] This was also the belief of William Penn in his establishment of the Holy Experiment. [74] However, while Paine sought to protect that religious liberty through defensive warfare, after negotiations with the Crown had failed, Penn secured religious freedom through his successful, personal rapport with the monarchs of his period. Therefore, both approaches must be perceived in the context of their personal and historical circumstances. Essentially then, Paine was a Quaker on the issue of pacifism, as far as his circumstances would permit and, in this sense, his type of pacifism was sincere.

One of Paine's last controversial articles for the *Pennsylvania Magazine* which appeared in August 1775, "An Occasional Letter on the Female Sex," was the first appeal for female rights issued in America. The English radical appears to equate the female's social condition with the bondage of slavery and in this respect it may be possible that he was advocating greater social and political responsibilities for American women after the anticipated separation from Britain. Like his anti-slavery appeal, this article is grounded in Paine's espousal of the Testimony on Equality which appears "within the Quaker meeting in the equal opportunity for all to take part regardless of age, sex or ability." [75]

Affronted in one country by polygamy,
which gives them their rivals for inseparable
companions; enslaved in another by
indisoluble ties, which often join the gentle to
the rude, and sensibility to brutality; Even in
countries where they may be esteemed most
happy they are . . . robbed of freedom of

17

> will by the laws, the slaves of opinion, which
> rules them with absolute sway, surrounded
> on all sides by judges who are at once their
> tyrants and seducers -- who does not feel
> for the tender sex? Yet such I am sorry to
> say is the lot of women over the whole earth.
> 76

Paine ends this appeal by requesting that his American brothers not deny their women "that public esteem which, after the esteem of one's self, is the sweetest reward of well-doing." [77] Once again we see Paine writing from his Quaker convictions. A deist would have been hard pressed to make an argument for womens' rights. For him, only the rights of independent people could be acknowledged and, in the deist's view , women were not and could not be independent beings; such a notion defied the law of nature and reason.

Paine's most comprehensive and effective articulation of the Revolutionary ideology, however, came in January 1776 after he had resigned from the editorship of the *Pennsylvania Magazine*. The effectiveness of "Common Sense" in mobilizing public support for the Revolutionary ideology was extraordinary. Paine's pamphlet "went through twenty-five editions and reached literally hundreds of thousands of readers in the single year 1776." Only three months after its initial publication roughly 150,000 copies of "Common Sense" had been sold in a population of approximately 1,580,000. [78]

There is little doubt among contemporary historians of the American Revolution that "Common Sense" provided the final and most direct impetus in the cause for independence. The most prominent of these historians have credited the influence of Newton, Locke, Milton, Sidney and Price as the primary influences on Paine's ideas as expressed in "Common Sense." [79] In fact, however, the predominant influence was that of Quakerism. The ideas set forth in the work are reflective of Quaker thought in four significant respects: 1) the articulation of the obligations and basis for civil government; 2) the incessant expression of pacifism; 3) a millennial spirit reminiscent of early Quakerism; and 4) the simplicity of style in which the pamphlet was written.

First, the influence of Penn, the political theorist of the Quakers, on the thought of Paine has been previously traced to their mutual residence in Sussex, England. This influence was instrumental in shaping Paine's ideas, as detailed in "Common Sense," on the obligations of civil government to society. Paine begins his piece by addressing this issue:

> Society is produced by our wants, goverment by
> our wickedness . . . Society in every state is a
> blessing, government in its best state is but a
> necessary evil . . .Here then is the origin and rise
> of government; namely, a mode rendered
> necessary by the inability of moral virtue to govern
> the world; here too is the design and end of
> government, Freedom and security. [80]

Similarly, William Penn, in his "One Project for the Good of England" (1679), makes the same distinction between loyalty to the state and loyalty to society. Penn encourages the establshment of civil government because of man's inability to reach consensus on moral/religious matters.

Furthermore, Penn, like Paine, views the obligation of government as the protection of civil interest:

> Scripture interprets [Religion] to be loving God
> above all, and our neighbors as ourselves; but
> practice teacheth us that too many merely resolve it
> into opinion and form . . . since 'tis so hard to
> disabuse men of their wrong apprehensions of
> religion . . . we must recur to some lower but
> true principle for the present. 'Tis this, that civil
> interest is the foundation and end of civil
> government, and thus: The good of the whole is
> the rise and end of government; but the good of
> the whole must

need be the interest of the whole, and consequently the interest of the whole is the reason and end of government. [81]

More significantly, Penn emphasizes the importance of government in securing a particular type of civil interest: religious liberty. In his advocacy of religious toleration Penn asserts that "the liberty of [conscience] in reference to faith and worship towards God . . . must not be denied" to those who "acknowledge the civil government under which they live." [82] Naturally, for Penn, the duty of the government was to secure this religious liberty.

Again, Paine draws his influence from Penn in his "Common Sense" assertion that "as to religion, I hold it to be the indispensable duty of government to protect all conscientious professors, thereof." Accordingly, Paine "fully and conscientiously believes" that the will of God insists on "a diversity of religious opinions." [83] In this sense, his republicanism reflects "an attempt to re-establish in politics and religion a lost harmony with the uniform, immutable, universal and eternal moral law." [84] Hence, the basis for Paine's republicanism, like Penn's, was predominantly Quaker in its attempt "to make the people's welfare -- the public good -- the exclusive end of government;" this was the fundamental value upon which the Revolutionary ideology was based. [85]

Second, in regard to his repeated expression of pacifism which constantly emerges throughout "Common Sense," Paine's advocacy of short-term war must be perceived in the context of his hope for peace in the long-term. He believed that only active pacifism, or a war for peace, would suffice since "every quiet method for peace had been ineffectual." [86] Furthermore, Paine claims that it is America's "duty to mankind at large, as well as to [the colonists] . . . to renounce the alliance" with England since any dependency on the monarchy "tends directly to involve [America] in European wars" against those "who would otherwise seek friendship." [87] He maintains that in a time when the "fate of war is uncertain", America, due to its undesired association to Britain, should "never suffer itself to be drained of inhabitants to support the British arms in either Asia, Africa or Europe." [88] Consequently, Paine urges the necessity of action to effect the cause of independence.

Paine's espousal of defensive warfare is the stumbling block upon which most historians dismiss any impact of a Quaker influence on him. [89] It has been previously illustrated, however, that there did exist a group of Free Quakers whose adherence to both the major body of principles of the Society and the cause for independence were sincere. In this respect, Paine's Revolutionary ideology was Quaker initiated and included a firm conviction in a future of peace.

Third, the content of "Common Sense" appears to be the political counter-part of the early Quaker religious proclamation tracts. This similarity is due to Paine's early exposure to these tracts, as previously mentioned, at his father's encouragement. The vocabulary of Biblical millennialism is of primary significance in the early Quaker tracts and in Paine's writing. These early Quaker pamphleteers, in their attempt to arouse the anticipation of their readers and prepare them for a new world, stressed that involvement in the millennial process was a personal responsibility to which everyone must attend.

William Dewsbury in his "True Prophecy of the Mighty Day of the Lord" (1655) calls on all men to share in a world struggle against pride and self-will, and suggests that by doing so they will be rewarded with life in a new world, another "Garden of Eden:"

> Stand faithful in [the Lord's] counsel, and walk in
> his power, everyone in your measure; and be bold
> in the Lord for you are the Army of the Lord God
> Almighty . . . in doing so you shall escape the
> wrath of God which is coming upon the children

> of disobedience in this nation for the Lord will
> make the earth as the Garden of Eden . . .
> Rejoice, rejoice! Ye saints and children of the
> Most High God, walk in his power and you shall
> walk as Kings upon the earth, and shall sing the
> new song that none can sing! [90]

Likewise Paine proclaims:

> We have it in our power to begin the world over
> again. The birthday of a new world is at hand . .
> . O ye that love mankind! Ye that dare oppose,
> not only the tyranny, but the tyrant, stand forth!
> Every spot of the old world is overrun with
> oppression . . .O! receive the fugitive, and
> prepare in time an asylum for mankind . . . for
> [the mission of American independence] is, in
> great measure, the cause of all mankind at large .
> . .The Almighty hath implanted in us these
> unextinguishable feelings for good and wise
> purposes. They are the guardians of his image in
> our hearts. [91]

Another aspect of the proclamation tract was "a message of
warning or an appeal to a particular group and situation." [92]
The warnings these tracts contained were primarily directed
"against corrupt administrators of the law." [93] Consistent with
this tradition, Dewsbury addresses the political leaders of
Cromwellian England:

> To you rulers of England you have seen the power
> of the Lord manifest on many that are in the place
> where you are, a cloud of witnesses: the bishops
> and the King, the lords and the late [Rump]
> Parliament, who professed the name of Christ but
> would not obey his counsel of their own hearts and
> improved their power for their own ends. But our
> righteous God hath overturned them to their
> everlasting shame and contempt. [94]

"Common Sense" serves as a fitting analogy to Dewsbury's
tract in its similar identification of the hypocrisy of England's

rule and its warning against self-centered corruption, by the king, of English law:

> I affirm that it would be policy in the King at this time to repeal the [Intolerable] acts, for the sake of reinstating himself in the government of the provinces, in order that he may accomplish by craft and subtlety, in the long run, what he cannot do by force and violence in the short run. Reconciliation and ruin are nearly related. [95]

Additionally, early Quaker proclamation tract writers utilized "Old Testament prophets to illustrate the sins of Israel" and thereby "bewail the state of England" in order to change public policy towards religious toleration. [96] Such is the case with Dewsbury who employs quotations from the Old Testament prophets Isaiah, Jeremiah and Ezekiel in condemning the luxurious lifestyle of the religious and political leaders of England. Accordingly, Dewsbury accuses these leaders of hypocrisy in their preference to "feed with the fat, and make prey for the people as the false prophets did" while simultaneously shunning these ministers of "the true religion." [97]

Similarly, Paine draws from the Old Testament prophet Gideon to legitimate his claim that monarchy and hereditary succession are against the will of the Almighty. Paine points out that Gideon, after having successfully "marched against [the Midianites] with a small army [of Jews] was requested to become King of Israel." However, Gideon, "in the piety of his soul replied, 'I will not rule over you, neither shall my son rule over you. The Lord shall rule over you!' " [98] Paine's subsequent "bewailment of the state of England" is a derivative of the fact that a human monarchy had long been established in the country with the result that "every spot of the old world is overrun with oppression, freedom hath been hunted and . . . England hath given her warning to depart." [99]

Finally, both pamphlets contain visions of the near or distant future; an essential characteristic of all early Quaker proclamation tracts. [100] Dewsbury informs his readers:

> The mighty day of the Lord is coming, and has
> appeared in the North of England and is arising
> toward the South; and shall overspread this nation
> and all nations of the world. [101]

"Common Sense" also offers a vision of America's near future:

> The birthday of a new world is at hand, and a race
> of men, perhaps as numerous as all Europe
> contains, are to receive their portion of freedom
> from the events of a few months. [102]

Clearly, Paine's "Common Sense," like the proclamation tracts of the early Quakers, delivers the most compact and incisive statement of the Quaker world view. Still, the content of Paine's pamphlet is only partial evidence of a strong Quaker influence; the style in which the piece was written shows the strong impact of Quaker thought on Paine's writing.

Fourth, in regard to the literary style of "Common Sense" Paine himself opens the work with the remark that he "offers nothing more than simple facts, plain arguments and common sense;"nothing could be more true. [103] American historians have often maintained that the work is unique in that Paine's "rhetoric was clear, simple and straightforward; his arguments rooted in the common experiences of a mass readership." [104] In this respect, Paine's style differed from those of contemporary pamphleteers who would frequently employ Latin, florid language, an ample amount of quotation from classical works and a host of artful literary devices in order to demonstrate their scholarship. [105] Moreover, the use of such literary devices as satire, elusive irony and flat parody by American political writers reflect the "stylistic modes associated with the great age of English pamphleteering" which "for all of their high self-consciousness of literary expression . . . were not great documents." [106] In this sense, Paine's "Common Sense" could not have been written by any English or American pamphleteer other than a Quaker.

The religiously-guarded education experienced by Paine, as previously mentioned, actively discouraged the learning of Latin or exposure to the classics and as well disuaded the Quaker pupil from imaginative literary devices and florid language. This fact explains the noticeable absence of those literary mechanisms in Paine's "Common Sense." More significant, "plainness of literary style was a desideratum with the Quakers," as demonstrated by the Dewsbury tract. The phrasing and vocabulary of these first Friends was adopted "from the English of the middle classes and from the Bible," a quality which is the hallmark of "Common Sense." [107] In short, "Common Sense," by virtue of its content and style, can only be regarded as the product of a "dyed-in-the-wool-Quaker."

Conclusion

The ideology of any socio-political movement is the composite of innumerable and diverse theological, social, political and economic influences. The American Revolution is a good illustration of this fact. Hence, to maintain that Quaker thought provided the exclusive influence on the ideology of the Revolution would be historically irresponsible. However, the backgrounds from which the American forefathers came to espouse the Revolutionary ideology were as diverse as the numerous influences which combined to create that ideology. In this respect, Thomas Paine's contribution to the '76 ideology was motivated by his strong Quaker background and convictions.

Being a product of his age, Paine eventually adopted the rationalism of the Enlightenment period. However, his later espousal of Jeffersonian deism was conditioned by some of the similarities it shared with Quaker thought: both placed a fundamental significance on the individual's right to private judgement in religious matters, a de-emphasis on the significance of the Scriptures in shaping religious conviction, opposition to the mediation of clergy between God and the individual and an emphasis on humanitarianism. Nevertheless, contemporary historians insist that Paine's Quakerism played a minimal, if any, role in his Revolutionary involvement, pointing to his belief in defensive warfare. [108] However, to single out pacifism as the sole test of Quaker conviction is to denigrate the very basis of Quaker thought itself, the Inner Light, which guides the individual in his search for religious and moral truth. Paine then, like his associates of the "Free Quaker milieu," was following the leading of his Inner Light in his conviction as to the rightness of the Revolutionary cause.

Finally, whatever his politico-religious preference was in later years, Paine's first socio-political writings reflect a uniquely Quaker configuration characterized by the triad of pacifism, equality and simplicity. Together with his ability to articulate simply the ideas behind the Revolution, the content of Paine's works are silent testimonies to the Quaker legacy of our nation.

Endnotes

[1] Gordon S. Wood, The Creation of the American Republic. (Chapel Hill, 1969), 46-74.

[2] Ibid., 15.

[3] See Seth B. Hinshaw, Quaker Influence on American Ideals (1976); and William W. Comfort, William Penn and Our Civil Liberties (1947)

[4] Arthur J. Mekeel, "The Founding Years," Friends in the Delaware Valley, edited by John M. Moore (Philadelphia, 1981), 39-42. At the time of the French and Indian War in 1756, the Quakers as a Society disassociated themselves from political involvement in Pennsylvania affairs, believing such participation to be inconsistent with their pacifist convictions. Also see Arthur J. Mekeel, The Relation of the Quakers to the American Revolution. (Washington D.C., 1979). Mekeel provides a detailed account, by colony, of Quaker political and military involvement, as well as non-involvement during the American Revolution. However, he does not indicate any strong Quaker influence on the ideology of the Revolution itself.

[5] See Frederick Tolles, Meeting House and Counting House. (Chapel Hill, 1948), 247-50. Tolles points out that although Benjamin Franklin was, and still is, often mistaken as the prototype of an honest Quaker, he espoused no religious convictions.

[6] George Chalmers, Francis Oldy's The Life of Thomas Paine. (London, 1793), 7; Moncure D. Conway, The Life of Thomas Paine. (2 vols., New York, 1892), I & II; Mary A. Best, Thomas Paine: Prophet and Martyr of Democracy. (New York, 1927), 8; Alfred O. Aldridge, Man of Reason. (New York, 1959), 14; Eric Foner, Tom Paine and Revolutionary America. (London, 1976), 33.

[7] Paine had bequeathed most of his belongings to a Mme. Bonneville who had cared for him in the last years of his life. Paine's personal papers were handed down to her son in whose St. Louis residence they were destroyed by fire.

[8] Howard H. Brinton, The Religious Philosophy of Quakerism. (Wallingford, Pa., 1973), 5-7.

[9] Rufus M. Jones, The Later Periods of Quakerism. (2 vols., London, 1921), I, 156-157.

[10] Best, Prophet & Martyr, 129; Chalmers, Oldy's Life of Paine, 7.

[11] This shift in environment was due, among other things, to the deaths of the first generation of leaders George Fox, William Penn and Robert Barclay accompanied by a decline in the missionary spirit.

[12] Quoted from "Age of Reason," The Writings of Thomas Paine, edited by Moncure D. Conway, (4 vols., New York, 1908), IV, 62.

[13] Howard H. Brinton, Quaker Education in Theory and Practice. (Wallingford, Pa., 1967), 45.

14 Samuel Edwards, Rebel! (New York, 1974), 7.

15 Jones, Later Periods, I , 33.

16 Thomas Paine, The Complete Writings of Thomas Paine, edited by Philip S. Foner (2 vols., New York, 1945), II , 1189; Best, Prophet & Martyr, 129; Conway, Life of Paine, II , 201. Conway claims that "in a profound sense Paine was George Fox himself." These assertions have been strongly opposed by Harry H. Clark, "An Historical Interpretation of Thomas Paine's Religion," University of California Chronicle (January, 1933), 59-60, and by Robert P. Falk, "Thomas Paine: Deist or Quaker?"Pennsylvania Magazine of History and Biography, 62 (1938): 52-63. Both Clark and Falk maintain that Paine was only slightly influenced by his Quaker upbringing and then only in his humanitarian outlook. Apart from this moral influence of Quakerism, it should be noted that both Clark and Falk emphasized Paine's deistical works, "Rights of Man" and "Age of Reason," apparently giving little consideration to the possibility of a transformation in Paine's thought in later life after his writing of "Common Sense."

17 Jones, Later Periods, I , 196.

18 Foner, Paine & Revolutionary America, 3; Aldridge, Man of Reason, 8.

19 William C. Braithwaite, The Second Period of Quakerism. (Cambridge, England, 1955), 457-64.

20 Walter H. Godfrey & J.M. Connell, At the Sign of the Bull, Lewes. (London, n.d.), 28.

21 David F. Hawke, Paine. (New York, 1974), 20; Aldridge, Man of Reason, 24; Edwards, Rebel!, 16; Conway, Life of Paine, I , 21. Paine married Ollive's daughter, Elizabeth, after the elder Quaker's death. The marriage was never consummated, due to the fact that Paine pitied, rather than loved the woman. Having been left with her father's business and no one to look after her, Elizabeth's need for a man was great. Paine agreed to the marriage since it would be mutually advantageous, he needing a place to live. In 1774, however, Paine left his wife, using the 35 pounds sterling retained in the marriage settlement to travel to America. He never returned to see Elizabeth, nor did he ever divorce her.

22 Sir Leslie Stephen & Sir Sidney Lee, "Thomas Rickman," Dictionary of National Biography. (London, 1917), XVI, 1152. Rickman's historical interest earned him the pseudonym "Clio", who in Greek mythology, was one of the nine muses which presided over literature, the arts and sciences. Clio was the Muse of History.

23 Proceedings of the White Hart Club, 1760-1770, in Godfrey & Connell, Sign of the Bull, 28.

24 Ibid.; Edwards, Rebel!, 15; Conway, Life of Paine, I , 2.

25 Caroline Robbins, The Eighteenth Centurey Commonwealthman. (Cambridge, Mass., 1959), 386.

26 Ibid., 10-13.

27 Ibid., 386.

28 Wood, Creation of the Republic, 15.

29 Calender of Home Office Papers of the Reign of George III, 1773-1775. (London, 1899), 39-42; Edwards, Rebel!, 16-17.

30 Aldridge, Man of Reason, 22; Paine, Writings, ed. Foner, II, 11-12; In "The Case of the Officers of Excise" Paine argues that an increase in wages would bring about greater efficiency and a tremendous increase in the revenue of the state. He warns against the evils resulting from inadequate salaries, cautioning that "poverty, in defiance of principle, begets a degree of meanness that will stoop to anything."

31 Walter J. Shelton, English Hunger and Industrial Disorders. (Toronto, 1973), 203. The cause of these riots was the financial deficit created by England's involvement in the Seven Year's War and the attempt by businessmen and employers to raise or lower wages, respectively, to protect their profits.

32 Leonard Krieger, "The Kings at Home: The Ascending Powers" in Felix Gilbert's The Norton History of Modern Europe. (New York, 1970), 749. John Wilkes was a member of Parliament who was prosecuted in 1763 for an article he wrote attacking the credibility of Lord Bute, the chief minister of George III. The publication of a similar article in 1768 resulted in Wilkes' expulsion from Parliament. Although Wilkes was subsequrntly elected to Parliament four times in succession, he was imprisoned for twenty-two months and prohibited from taking his seat in the Commons. This incident raised the revolutionary issue of the political rights of the electors. "Wilkes and Liberty" became the political catchall as the Commonwealth movement came to be embraced by the unprivileged, unenfranchised and unpropertied members of English society.

33 Paine, Writings, ed. Foner, II, 464. Paine claimed that his experience in London as a lobbyist placed him in a unique position "to see into the numerous and various distresses which the weight of taxes even at that time of the day occasioned."

34 Harry E. Wildes, William Penn. (New York, 1974), 101.

35 Ibid., 127, 133.

36 Tolles, Meeting House, 13.

37 Ibid.

38 Braithwaite, Second Period of Quakerism, 179.

39 Wildes, Penn, 101; Mark Lower, A Compendioius History of Sussex. (2 vols., London, 1870), II, 229.

40 Rufus Jones, The Quakers in the American Colonies. (London, 1911), 566.

41 Isaac Sharpless, Quaker Experiment in Government. (Philadelphia, 1902), 234; Sharpless maintains that one-fifth of the "adult male Friends in

Philadelphia had joined the American army or had taken places under the Revolutionary government" at the outbreak of war. Considering that there were about 5000 Friends in the Philadelphia area in 1766, Sharpless is speaking of approximately 200 who were disowned in the first years of the war. See also Robert Proud, History of Pennsylvania. (2 vols. Philadelphia, 1798), II, 278, 339; and Mekeel, Relation of Quakers, 132, 169, 335.

[42] Mekeel, Relation of Quakers, 289.

[43] Ibid., 285.

[44] Junior League of Philadelphia, The Free Quakers and Their Meeting House. (Philadelphia, 1976), 3; Mekeel, Relation of Quakers, 286. The fact that there were 50,000 Quakers in America out of a population of 1,580,000 during the Revolution gives one an idea of how small the Free Quaker movement was. According to Mekeel, a small group of Free Quakers developed in New England in 1783. However, there was not as strong a feeling of alienation among the New England Friends as prevailed in Philadelphia and by 1795 most of these separatists had rejoined the main body of the Society (See Mekeel, Relation of Quakers, 286-89)

[45] Paine journied to France in 1781 in search of further financial relief for the American cause. After he returned later the same year he lived in Bordentown, New Jersey, and, briefly, on his farm in New Rochelle, New York. He left America in 1787, travelling to Europe in order to pursue the revolutionary cause of France and did not return to this country until 1802.

[46] Hawke, Paine, 39; Aldridge, Man of Reason, 46. Matlack had been disowned in 1765 for un-sound business practices (Mekeel, Relation of Quakers, 290, n. 2)

[47] Christopher Marshall, Passages from the Diary of Christopher Marshall, edited by William Duane (Philadelphia, 1849), 33; Richard A. Ryerson, The Revolution Is Now Begun. (Philadelphia, 1978), 131, 229; Hawke, Paine, 102. Christopher Marshall had been disowned in 1751 for "insufficiency of acknowledgement in the charge of intimate association with men engaged in forgery (Mekeel, Relation of Quakers, 81).

[48] Mekeel, Relation of Quakers, 288.

[49] A. M. Stackhouse, Patriot and Soldier. (n.p., 1910), 92. During his tenure as clerk to the Secretary of the Congress, Matlack engrossed the Declaration of Independence.

[50] Conway, Life of Paine, I , 94. In one of his letters, dated October 10, 1777, Matlack, acting as Secretary to the Assembly, informs Paine that he is requested to join the Continental Army at Valley Forge so that the Assembly can "obtain more regular and constant intelligence of the proceeding of G. Washington's army." Matlack completes the letter with an interesting personal allusion which reflects his mutual discouragement over the Society's pacifist stance: "I expect to send you a copy of the Testimony of the late Yearly Meeting . . . 'tis a poor thing." Here, Matlack refers to

the testimony of the 1777 Yearly Meeting which dealt with the Society's decision to "stand firm" in their adherence to the Peace Testimony.

[51] Edwards, Rebel!, 40.

[52] Aldridge, Man of Reason, 47. This fact is also reflected in the abundant correspondence between Paine and Greene after the former's return to civilian life. The correspondence can be found in Paine, Writings, ed. Foner, II.

[53] Theodore Thayer, Nathanael Greene, Strategist of the American Revolution. (New York, 1960), 20.

[54] Ibid., 33.

[55] Greene quoted in ibid., 40-41.

[56] Nathanael Greene, The Papers of General Nathanael Greene, edited by Richard Showman, (5 vols, Chapel Hill, 1976), II, 183-184. In a letter to his brother, dated October 27, 1777, Greene writes: "The Quakers voluntarily lent General Howe 5,000 pounds sterling at his arrival in this city [Phila.] . . . The Friends say they wish G. Washington's army was cut into pieces that there would be peace. These are lamb like wishes, and breathe that universal benevolence they profess for all mankind!"; See also East Greenwich (Rhode Island) Monthly Meeting Minutes: 4 mo./5/1777 quoted in Showman, Papers of Greene, II, 104, n. 4.

[57] "American Crisis #1" in Paine, Writings, ed. Conway, I , 170.

[58] "American Crisis #3" in ibid., I , 206-20.

[59] Ibid.

[60] See Daniel J. Borstin, The Lost World of Thomas Jefferson. (Chicago, 1948); Gustov A. Koch, Republican Religion. (New York, 1933).

[61] Chester C. Maxey, "Thomas Paine," Political Philosophers. (New York, 1938), 390-91.

[62] Edwards, Rebel!, 28. Although Paine became friendly with Franklin, Jefferson and Priestly during his first two years in Philadelphia, "he knew none of them well enough, as yet, to call upon any ideas other than his own."

[63] Thomas Drake, Quakers and Slavery in America. (New Haven, 1950), 25; Mekeel, "The Founding Years," in Moore, Friends in Delaware Valley, 31. Woolman's publication, "some Considerations on the Keeping of Negroes" played a significant role in convincing the Friends that they should abandon slaveholding.

[64] David B. Davis, The Problem of Slavery in the Age of Revolution, 1770-1823. (Ithaca, 1975), 230; Jones, Quakers in the American Colonies, 511-18. The Quakers of Germantown (Penna.) Monthly Meeting had presented the first group protest against chattel slavery as early as 1688. The first official Quaker statement against slaveholding appeared in the minutes of the Philadelphia Yearly Meeting in 1758 although that body did not prescribe disownment for the keeping of slaves until 1776. Similarly,

English Quakers Samuel and John Fothergill preached against slavery in the 1750s, abetting "future English Quaker abolitionists" as well as laying the foundations "for more secular and radical abolitionism" in Englans. (See Mekeel, "The Founding Years," in Moore, Friends in Delaware Valley, 44).

[65] Paine, Writings, ed. Conway, I , 7.

[66] Davis, Problem of Slavery, 213, 251-52.

[67] Philadelphia Yearly Meeting Minutes, 1758: 121-122.

[68] Paine, Writings, ed. Conway, I , 65-66. Also interesting to note in this passage is Paine's implication of the immanence of God, a conviction not held by the deist.

[69] Ibid., 40.

[70] Ibid.

[71] Ibid., 56.

[72] Ibid., 55.

[73] Ibid., 56-57.

[74] William Penn, "The Frame of Government of the Province of Pennsylvania (1682)" in Edwin Bronner, William Penn, 17th Century Founding Father. (Lebanon, Pa., 1975), 13.

[75] Brinton, Religious Philosophy, 132. Naturally, the Society's equal treatment of women experienced a gradual evolution, as did many of the social testimonies of Friends. However, Quakers from the time of their establishment highly encouraged females to participate in religious affairs, social reform and most significantly, the open ministry. Paine's article is unmistakenly a reflection of his Quaker background since the Friends were the only non-conformist sect which permitted such equal treatment of females.

[76] Paine, Writings, ed. Conway, I , 61.

[77] Ibid., 63-64.

[78] Eric Foner, Paine & Revolutionary America, 79. Consumer statistics cannot account for the number of people who actually read "Common Sense." However, these statistics can be considered the most accurate barometer for the popularity of Paine's pamphlet for the time period. Moreover, Foner maintains that "Common Sense" reached not only the literate but was "read to all ranks," including the illiterate.

[79] Ibid., 6-12. Eric Foner credits the influence of Newtonian Science and the political thought of Richard Price on Paine's ideology; Gordon Wood in his Creation of the American Republic, 48-49, believes that Sidney and Milton, among others, influenced the thought of American Whigs like Paine; Bernard Bailyn, Ideological Origins of the American Revolution. (Cambridge, 1967), 27-30, credits Locke for the primary influence on American radicals like Paine.

[80] Paine, Writings, ed. Conway, I , 69-71.

[81] William Penn, "One Project for the Good of England," in The Complete Works of William Penn, edited by Joseph Besse (2 vols., London, 1726), II, 682.

[82] William Penn, "A Persuasive to Moderation to Church Dissenters" in Works of Penn, II, 729.

[83] Paine, Writings, ed. Conway, I , 108.

[84] Wood, Creation of Republic, 60.

[85] Ibid., 55.

[86] Paine, Writings, ed. Conway, I , 88. Paine is here referring to the colonial attempt to initiate peace by offering the Olive Branch Petition of 1775 which was rejected by George III.

[87] Ibid.

[88] Ibid., 87.

[89] See Robert Falk, "Thomas Paine and the Attitude of the Quakers to the American Revolution." Pennsylvania Magazine of History and Biography, 63 (1939): 302-10, and Norman Sykes, "Thomas Paine" in The Social and Political Ideas of Some Representative Thinkers of the Revolutionary Era, V, 129. Both historians argue that any Quaker influence on Paine is negated by his involvement militarily in the Revolution.

[90] William Dewsbury, "True Prophecy of the Mighty Day of the Lord" in Hugh Barbour & Arthur O. Roberts, Early Quaker Writings, 1650-1700. (Grand Rapids, Michigan, 1973), 101-102. Dewsbury was one of the first religious Seekers to join George Fox in 1652. He became a prominent member of the Valiant Sixty, agroup of itinerant ministers initiated by Fox to carry our the Quaker Lamb's War by spreading truth to all parts of England. Dewsbury in this particular prophetic tract condemns the Commonwealth government of Oliver Cromwell and beseeches his fellow countrymen to prepare for the millennium.

[91] Paine, Writings, ed. Conway, I , 88-119.

[92] Luella M. Wright, The Literary Life of the Early Friends, 1650-1725. (New York, 1932), 128.

[93] Ibid.

[94] Dewsbury, "True Prophecy," in Barbour and Roberts, Early Quaker Writings, 102.

[95] Paine, Writings, ed. Conway, I , 95.

[96] Wright, Literary Life, 128.

[97] Dewsbury, "True Prophecy," in Barbour and Roberts, Early Quaker Writings, 98.

[98] Paine, Writings, ed. Conway, I , 77.

[99] Ibid., 101.

[100] Wright, Literary Life, 128.

[101] Dewsbury, "True Prophecy," in Barbour and Roberts, Early Quaker Writings, 93.

[102] Paine, Writings, ed. Conway, I , 119.

[103] Ibid., I , 84.

[104] Eric Foner, Paine & Revolutionary America, xvi.

[105] W. E. Woodward, Tom Paine, America's Godfather. (New York, 1945), 68.

[106] Bailyn, Ideological Origins, 9-12.

[107] Wright, Literary Life, 188-189.

[108] See Falk, "Paine & Attitude of Quakers," 302-10 and Sykes, "Thomas Paine," Social & Political Ideas, V, 29.

Chapter 2
"The Fighting Quaker": Nathanael Greene's Conflict of Conviction

The War for American Independence tested the nation's ideal of individual conduct. Patriotism assumed a variety of forms ranging from payment of war taxes to direct participation in the military engagement of the war. Conversely, there were also those Americans who took an active part in opposing the cause of independence by supporting, militarily or financially, the mother country. There were still others who, out of respect for their religious affiliation (i.e., most notably the Society of Friends), maintained a neutral position during the conflict. None of these commitments were made without a strong consideration of the implications each one held, particularly those involving independence from Great Britain. To choose such a course carried with it obligations to make decisions, to take risks and to accept the consequences. Inevitably the desire for independence threatened order in an individual's life, instigating change, conflict and insecurity.

This choice of individual conduct and the conflict of conviction that, in many cases, accompanied it affected those who entered the Continental Army as private soldiers as well as those who served in the high command of that body. One of these individuals, Nathanael Greene of Rhode Island, serves as a fine example of a Quaker who pitted political allegiance against religious conviction in joining the ranks of Washington's army and suffered a prolonged personal conflict for having done so.

Greene was believed to be "the greatest military genius produced by the American Revolution." In fact, Washington is said to have considered the Rhode Island general as the "first of all [his subordinate officers] in point of military knowledge and ability" and as the most qualified successor to his own command. 1 Greene's military record speaks for itself. After the Battle of Lexington, Congress promoted him from an officer of the Rhode Island militia to Major General in the Continental Army. He served with distinction in the battles of Trenton, Brandywine and Germantown before being entrusted with the difficult position of Quartermaster General at the Valley Forge encampment. Later, the Rhode Island general was to lead the Continental Army in the Southern theater of war. Despite the superior forces of the British, Greene succeeded in driving the enemy out of the Carolinas and Georgia. This action compelled Cornwallis to move north where he was ultimately obliged to surrender at Yorktown.

These military successes were, at best, a mixed blessing for Greene who, being raised a Quaker, wrestled with a fundamental ideological dilemma: "Was it possible to balance an allegiance to the state without deviating from the principles of the Society of Friends?" Ultimately Greene found himself caught in a conflict of conviction, being unable to reconcile the two. His decision to go to war must have been an extremely difficult one to make as it involved not only religious considerations but financial, political and intellectual interests all of which were critical to his self-esteem. Still, Greene's "Quaker conscience" strongly influenced his decision making process between the years 1770-1786 as evidenced by his writings and actions during that period.

Nathanael Greene's decision to go to war was conditioned, in part, by the spiritual transformation of eighteenth-century Quakerism itself. During the first part of the eighteenth-century,

36

Quakers began to find the Society's testimonies on a religiously-guarded lifestyle much too rigid. Despite the Society's attempt to reinforce its testimonies on simplicity of lifestyle, urging Friends to "moderate or renounce their absorbing interest in property, political office and power," its pleas fell on deaf ears. By the 1750s material prosperity had claimed a higher priority among Friends than a truly religious character. The situation worsened with the advent of the French-Indian war, when Quakers throughout the American colonies were compelled to choose between their pacifist convictions and their political involvements. Under these circumstances, a group of Quaker reformers sought to affect a spiritual reformation within the Society. Inspired by the preaching of an itinerant Quaker minister from England, Samuel Fothergill, in 1755, these reformers urged their respective yearly meetings to tighten their discipline and raise barriers between Friends and the world in order to purge the Society of all corrupt influence. This movement had a profound impact on Pennsylvania Friends, in particular, who withdrew in large numbers from their colony's legislature. [2] In Rhode Island, however, this spiritual reformation occurred more gradually.

By the mid-eighteenth-century Quakerism had become quite popular in the Rhode Island colony extending itself from the Friends' initial stronghold in Newport, north to Providence and Smithfield, across the bay to East Greenwich and from there to the Connecticut border at Westerly. [3] Friends were regarded as the leaders of their communities because of their political and economic involvements. Many were prosperous merchants who also held influential posts in the New England Yearly Meeting and, hence, were "well known in Rhode Island for their upright lives which were conspicuous in their social and business actions. " [4] Friends had also established a respectable reputation in the political life of the colony. Because Rhode Island had no requirement on swearing oaths, Quakers held political office at all levels. Despite the urging of Fothergill, in 1755, to withdraw from government, there was no immediate change in the political participation of Rhode Island's Quakers. Unlike their

Pennsylvania bretheren, these Friends did not hold government office as an independent party and they concerned themselves with matters that were well outside of any conflict with the Society's testimonies. [5] While Rhode Island Friends did not experience the blatant contradiction between political practice and pacifist conviction that characterized the circumstances of the Pennsylvania Quakers, they were not without their worldly influences.

Quaker piety was easily diluted by the influences of Rhode Island's many religious denominations. Although the Quakers and Baptists composed the largest congregations in the colony, Anglicans, Moravians, Congregationalists, Jews and even Catholics had also established themselves there. [6] Their mutual influence served to challenge Quaker orthodoxy, particularly in matters of education and lifestyle. Newport Friends especially came to believe that "piety need not be at odds with learning" and strayed from their religiously-guarded educations in order to satisfy their intellectual curiosity. And in a religiously-tolerant colony such as Rhode Island, theology was one of the more popular topics for intellectual discourse. Samuel Hopkins and Ezra Stiles, two of the most brilliant minds in pre-Revolutionary America and the local Congregationalist ministers, often encouraged Friends to enter into such a discussion. Friends also enhanced their worldly knowledge through reading. When a wealthy Quaker merchant, Abraham Redwood, endowed a library for 500 pounds sterling, many of the Newport Friends discovered that they had more pleasing alternatives to Fox's *Journal* and Barclay's *Apology*. In their attempt to "cut a fine figure among the well-to-do," some Friends lost their interest in egalitarianism and the plain style altogether. These "Quaker Grandees," as they were called, shocked rural Friends who adhered to the pietistic preferences for an unlearned, spirit-filled way of life. [7] Not surprisingly, these rural Friends formed the core of a spiritual reform movement in New England Yearly Meeting. Their movement would gradually gain strength in the 1760s and prevail in the 1770s after the death of the older, more tolerant generation. [8]

Initially, Samuel Fothergill's visit to Rhode Island in 1755 resulted in New England Yearly Meeting's adoption of a requirement that their subordinate meetings write specific answers to each query on a member's behavior and on the state of the meeting, this in order to inform the parent body of a particular meeting's commitment to Quaker testimonies. [9] Five years later, in 1760, the Yearly Meeting revised its rules of conduct along the lines of the English Quakers. By 1770, with the passing of the older, more tolerant generation of Quakers, the new generation of reformers came into power within New England Yearly Meeting and the discipline became more severe.

Under their leadership, Rhode Island's monthly meetings were directed to investigate persons who failed to attend meeting regularly, those who neglected to observe the Society's social testimonies and those whose conduct might bring the Society into disrepute. Their efforts were successful. Between 1770 and 1775, in Rhode Island Monthly Meeting alone, the number of dealings for disciplinary action more than tripled the total number of cases in the preceding five years. Discipline became even more severe during the Revolutionary War as New England Yearly Meeting insisted on a strict compliance with the Society's Peace Testimony. Under these circumstances, young Quakers, especially, may have found it easier to break the discipline of the Society when their meetings disowned so many members anyway. [10] Moreover, disownment from the Society did not have as great an impact in a religiously-diverse environment as it would have in a more homogeneous society. Those who were disowned could easily find companionship -- spiritual or other -- among Rhode Island's other denominations let alone their disowned Quaker bretheren. And to be sure, they had a lot of company as one of the overall effects of this spiritual reformation was to depopulate the Society of Friends. [11] Nathanael Greene was a victim of this spiritual transformation.

Born July 27, 1742 in the village of Potowomut, Warwick, Greene was raised in a strictly Quaker household. His father, Nathanael Sr., was a Quaker minister and the "spiritual leader of the East Greenwich Friends meeting." [12] Being a rural Friend, the elder Greene was orthodox in his beliefs, one contemporary having described him as a "fanatic who brooked no compromise with the world, the flesh or the devil." His conduct and dress also exemplified those of a "dyed-in-the-wool Quaker whose broad brim[med] [hat] and cut-a-way [clothes], high collared and stiff, were always of the most sanctimonious fashion" and whose life "had no softening "except for the "gentle 'thee' and 'thou' of Quaker speech." [13] Accordingly the father was "unsparingly severe" toward his "gay-tempered son, Nathanael." [14]

Despite the father's insistence that all eight of his sons should receive nothing more than a religiously-guarded, elementary education -- so they could work at the family forge -- Nathanael managed to circumvent those plans in order to receive quite a worldly education. Apparently a Scotsman by the name of Maxwell served as the young Greene's tutor, introducing him to Latin and the political commentaries of Locke and Hume. As an adolescent Greene, who was quickly becoming "a worldling Quaker," further enhanced his education through frequent trips to Newport. [15] These sojourns threw the youngster into the company of Ezra Stiles, a leader of the Great Awakening and a minister of the Second Congregational Church at Newport. In the 1750s Stiles was considered the chief of American scholars and he would emerge, later, as the hero of the growing nationalist movement to save the principle of religious liberty in America. Greene was attracted to the Congregationalist minister by these qualities and spent considerable time with him whenever he visited Newport. Not surprising, it was Stiles who introduced the Quaker adolescent to John Locke's "Essay on Human Understanding" as well as his own work entiled "Christian Union." [16] While the former tract emphasized the political role of the individual in society, the latter called for an ecumenical

union among the various Protestant denominations i
Both, however, challenged the orthodoxy of th
Friends and left Greene with a question of where ...ɔ ιoyalties
should rest; with Quakerism or with the secular spirit of the
times?

This dilemma manifested itself, during the period 1770-1775
in a correspondence Greene conducted with Samuel Ward Jr., the
son of a successful Newport merchant and a student at the College
of Rhode Island. Greene, in his late twenties, used the
correspondence to conduct an intellectual discourse. Here he
discusses a number of ethical questions and, in the process,
discloses his own moral philosophy. Most revealing though, is
the ambivalent attitude he maintains regarding his religious
convictions; something which is indicative of the tensions he
experienced between his Quaker upbringing and more secular
ideas. In September 1771, for example, Greene exalts the Quaker
doctrine of the Inner Light, encouraging Ward to "seek the good
in all men" and in doing so to "fix in yourself right ideas of
benevolence, humanity, integrity and truth." [17] Yet only a year
earlier, in September 1770, Greene questioned the motive of such
a "religious duty," claiming that "all our religious dispositions
and moral conduct are selfish acts" based on a "desire to promote
our own happiness" and to "obtain our own salvation." [18]
Similarly, in August 1772, Greene writes admiringly of the
Quaker simplicity he knew as a youth: "Plainness and Simplicity
of manners stript of all the paint and ornament of policy is what I
ever admired, it wins the affection by the force of its persuasion."
[19] Later that year, however, Greene contradicts these sentiments.
In a letter to Ward dated October 9, 1772, he denounces the
"plainness and simplicity" of his Quaker education as it served to
"cry down literature as a vain philosophy." He concludes that this
"constrained manner of education" has proved "a fine nursery of
ignorance and superstition instead of piety." [20] These
contradictions in Greene's philosophy became heightened during
the Revolutionary era.

Having the greatest degree of self-rule of any of the American colonies, Rhode Island had the most to lose in England's attempt to control her trade. Fierce opposition to the crown's policies began in Newport, in 1764, when the Sugar Act was levied. Subsequently, Rhode Islanders engaged in repeated measures of defiance, including the burning of the British custom sloop *Liberty* in July 1769, the torching of the British revenue schooner *Gaspee* in Warwick in 1772 and the holding of a "Tea Party" in Providence Market Square on March 2, 1775. Before the first shots of the war were fired at Lexington, in April 1775, the Rhode Islanders had achieved a united front against the British government. Even the political factions of Hopkins and Ward, which had divided the colony's legislature, suppressed their differences in order to endorse a series of political measures against the oppressive acts of the crown. [21] When war did come the Rhode Island legislature called for the raising of an army of 1,500 men and, within the year, renounced all allegiance to King George III.

Such measures were too severe for the Rhode Island Quakers who, in accordance with the Society's attempt at spiritual reform, began to withdraw from political office in an attempt to bear witness to the Peace Testimony. Although they were exempted from military service by laws passed during the two preceding inter-colonial wars, Rhode Island Quakers were subject to indirect services. [22] But when Friends refused to render even these indirect services, failing to "contribute their equal and necessary proportion for the defense of their [colony's] rights," the Assembly revoked their exemption. [23] From 1776 on, many of those Friends who refused to comply in any way with the war effort experienced the seizure of their goods for the use of the army. Several members of the Greene's East Greenwich Monthly Meeting suffered for their non-compliance, but Nathanael Jr. was not among them. [24]

Nathanael Greene's patriotism was initially stirred by economic considerations, in particular the British attempt to deprive him of his own property. By the 1760s the Greene family was becoming one of the more respected merchant families of Rhode Island. They had inherited from the family patriarch, Jabez Greene who had settled in the colony during the late seventeenth century, extensive properties in the towns of Warwick and North Kingstown. These holdings, which included a wharf, sawmills, warehouses and forges, were enlarged by Nathanael's father who, by 1763, was the second highest taxpayer in Warwick. [25] In 1768 the young Greene was entrusted with supervising the family ironworks at Coventry but it was not until 1772, when Greene's own property was attacked by the British, that he became involved in the Revolutionary movement.

On February 17, 1772 the infamous British schooner *Gaspee* intercepted Greene's sloop, the *Fortune,* in the Narragansett Bay. Like many of the other Rhode Island sloops which violated the British navigation acts by smuggling goods across the bay, the *Fortune* contained 12 hogsheads of rum and several sacks of brown sugar aboard. Lieutenant William Dudingston, the Royal Customs Inspector who captured Greene's sloop, had the *Fortune* towed into Newport, its owner to be tried in the admiralty court of Rhode Island. [26] Four months later, as Greene prepared to take the Inspector to court over the seizure of his property, the *Gaspee* was set afire, Dudingston barely escaping. A commission was appointed by the Crown to investigate the incident. During the hearings a British officer of the *Gaspee* accused Greene of leading the attack. Although the allegation proved to be false, it served to push the Rhode Island Quaker further along the path to war. [27]

The British seizure of the *Fortune* and the commission hearings which followed the destruction of the *Gaspee* marked a major turning point in Nathanael Greene's life. At a period of time when the term "right" was used interchangeably with "property" and the "pursuit of happiness,"the *Gaspee* affair could have only served to threaten Greene's political as well as economic rights. [28] Prior to 1772 he had enjoyed many rights which he had taken for granted. He had never really been affected by the constraining Iron Act as a forgemaster, nor had his commercial activities been restricted by the navigation acts as a small merchant. Consequently, Greene had little cause to involve himself in the colonial protests against England's mercantilist policies. None of his writings, prior to 1772, suggest any displeasure with Crown authority. However, the economic loss Greene incurred by the seizure of his sloop was severe enough to affect a sharp change in his attitude toward Great Britain. Additionally, popular resentment among Rhode Islanders towards royal authority was triggered by Greene's loss; an attitude that resulted in the destruction of the *Gaspee*. Just as other Rhode Islanders made Greene's cause their own, so too did Greene begin to understand their cause.

By 1773 the Quaker from East Greenwich became obssessed with the protection of American liberty against what he perceived to be the arbitrary power of the British government. Writing of the Crown's investigation of the *Gaspee* affair, Greene denounces the procedure as an "attack on every lover of Liberty in America." [29] The British closing of the Port of Boston was greeted with a much more bitter castigation of government policy. After learning of the imposition of the Intolerable Acts in 1774 Greene writes: "The priviledges and liberties of the people will be trampled to death by the prerogatives of the Crown . . . and that once wise and virtuous Parliament, but now wicked and weak Assembly, lends an assisting hand to accomplish these hellish schemes." [30] Later that year Greene donated 2 pounds sterling 8 shillings to the city of Boston for provisions and foodstuffs and joined in the formation of a colonial militia, the Kentish Guards. [31] But Greene would not be limited to these modest contributions. As the movement for independence continued to unfold he became an integral part of that cause. After the Rhode Island Assembly learned of the first military engagements at Lexington and Concord, in May 1775, it appointed Greene as "Brigadier General of the Rhode Island Army."[32] Greene accepted; the Quaker from East Greenwich was going to war. In a half-hearted attempt to explain his decision to his wife, Catharine, Greene wrote:

> It had been happy for me if I could have lived a private life in peace and plenty, enjoying all the happiness that results from a well-tempered society founded on mutual esteem. But the injury done my country . . . calls me forth to defend our common rights and repel the bold invaders of the Sons of Freedom. The cause is the cause of God and man.
> I am determined to defend my rights and maintain my freedom or sell my life in the attempt; and I hope the righteous God that rules the world will bless the armies of America. [33]

Greene, in his own mind, was attempting to elevate the movement for Independence to a Divine mission. Still, the Rhode Islander's assertion that the Continental cause "is the cause of God" does not square with his "hope [that] the righteous God . . . will bless the armies of America." The language is couched with an uncertainty indicative of a man who lacks confidence in his religious convictions. The major obstacle here was a Quaker tendency toward pacifism. This point is reinforced by Greene's sentiments shortly before his death in 1786. Although he still insisted that war "was ever a business of necessity, being fully authorized from nature and reason," the former Brigadier General admitted that he was "averse to it from its being opposite my temper and feelings" and that pacifism was a principle that he "inherently valued." [34] In 1775, however, Greene had placed a higher priority on his economic freedom and to a political allegiance that would secure that freedom for him. Thus, he prepared to fight a two-pronged battle; against the British and against his own religious convictions.

Throughout the war Greene struggled to place his patriotism above whatever feelings he still maintained for the Religious Society of Friends. When the Continental Congress issued paper money, in 1776, to finance the war, Friends refused to use it as the currency supported a violent cause. Greene was shocked at their "effrontery" and predicted that "this line of conduct [could not] fail of drawing down the resentment of the people upon them." The Quakers, he feared, would "smart for their folly." [35] After his arrival in Pennsylvania, in 1777, Greene castigated the Quakers bitterly for adopting a position of neutrality in the conflict. For Greene, as for many others who served in the Continental Army, non-compliance with the American cause undoubtedly meant loyal support for the British. [36] According to Greene the "villinous Quakers are employed upon every quarter to serve the enemy . . . they are poisoning everybody" and deserve to be confined. Simultaneously, the Rhode Island general reaffirmed his loyalty to the "loud calls of [his] country, to the peace, liberty and happiness of millions."[37] Greene's correspondence, during the year 1777, continued to detail the "treasonous" acts of the Society of Friends, though most of these accounts appear to be based on rumor as little evidence is given of a personal encounter with such offenders. [38] Not surprisingly, it was during this year that Greene officially severed his ties with the Society of Friends, requesting to be "put from under the care of East Greenwich Meeting for the future." [39]

Greene had become discouraged by the refusal of the Society of Friends to comply with the American war effort. Consequently, he permitted his patriotism to usurp a higher place in his loyalties than a confused, but still existent, set of religious values. It was with these mixed feelings that the Rhode Islander accepted the commission of Quartermaster General at the Valley Forge encampment, during the winter of 1777-1778. The responsibility was a great one with little prospect of success. Greene would have to provision the Continental Army -- a provincial band of 12,000 ill-equipped backwoodsmen and militiamen -- in spite of the non-compliance of the local inhabitants and the threat of attack by a much better trained and well-supplied fighting force of 20,000 British redcoats. [40] The hardship he would suffer, being exposed to starvation, disease and death, would be too difficult to bear for a man without faith. Greene attempted to fill this void by attaching himself to the

Reverend John Murray, a Universalist minister whose "talents and morals [had], early on, earned [Greene's] esteem." [41]

Universalism, itself, was the most anti-Calvinistic doctrine, being even more radical than Quakerism, and undoubtedly provided Greene with a feeling of total liberation from the constraints of pacifism or an after life. Accordingly, Greene appointed Murray the chaplain of his Rhode Island regiment in February 1778; despite the protestations of other regimental chaplains at Valley Forge. [42] Apparently the New England Quaker was attempting to replace the religion of his youth with a similar theology as their is some indication that Greene was very sympathetic toward Universalism or at least toward the views of Murray. [43]

Regardless of his attempts to extricate himself from any association with the Society of Friends though, Greene's "Quaker conscience" would not permit him the peace of mind he sought. Records of some of the Valley Forge families maintain that Greene, along with other local Quakers, "met regularly for worship at the house of Isaac Walker [since] a hospital had been established in the Valley meetinghouse . . . near the encampment." [44] There are also indications that Greene began to question his involvement in the war during his service at Valley Forge. Writing to Commander-in-Chief George Washington, in 1778, the Rhode Island general displays his disillusionment with the novelty of a patriotic cause. According to Greene, he and the other officers had "always flattered [themselves] that a love of liberty and a thirst for military glory were such predominant principles that there would never be want." However, under the present hardships he finds that "the spirit of patriotism and the splendor of military glory vanish into nothing" as he has been "obliged to sacrifice all the comforts of life, for empty sounds only which are the creatures of a day and then sink into contempt the remainder of life."[45] No longer do we see the burning desire to place liberty above personal concerns, as indicated in Greene's earlier writings. Instead, one is curious to know whether or not the "contempt" Greene might have felt for the "remainder of life" was based on the decision he made to place political allegiance and the violence it involved above the Quaker values he learned as a child. Although this issue is subject to interpretation, one thing is clear: Greene's subsequent treatment of the Quakers was directed by a much more sympathetic attitude than he demonstrated prior to 1778.

Acting as commander of the Continental forces in the South, Greene proved to be compassionate in his actions towards Southern Friends, many of whom had been deeply scarred by the war. In 1781, after the Battle of Guilford Courthouse in North Carolina, Greene appealed to the Friends to care for the wounded, maintaining that he knew of "no order of people more remarkable for the exercise of humanity and benevolence." The Quakers promised to oblige with this request in spite of the depradations they had suffered at the hands of both the Continental and British troops. [46] That same year when two itinerant Quaker ministers from Pennsylvania requested to "pass amongst [Greene's] men" in order to preach amongst their [southern] bretheren," Greene complied, stating that he held a "good opinion of the people of [their]profession, being bred and educated among them." Greene gave them the pass on the condition that his army received "the good wishes of the Quakers" as he believed that the army "wish[ed] to serve them upon all occasions not inconsistent with the public welfare." [47] Consistent with his beliefs, Greene did protect the Quakers during the southern campaign. When he received reports from South Carolina, for example, that Friends there were being mistreated by Continental soldiers because of their refusal for provisioning, the Rhode Island general assured those Friends of their protection by conducting an investigation into the matter. [48]

Greene never did completely reconcile his conflict of conviction between his Quaker values and his worldly desires. This may be due to the fact that he never had the opportunity for reflection that old age affords an individual. Greene died suddenly at the age of forty-four, shortly after the war had ended, leaving very little evidence in his writings as to his religious convictions in those last years of life. The historian can only speculate that Greene's conflict of conviction continued to plague him for the remainder of his life. Although he had planned to lead the life of a southern plantation owner,"dividing the year between Rhode Island and Georgia," his Quaker egalitarianism would not permit him to rest easy with owning the slaves required to cultivate that plantation. He even admitted that "nothing could be said in the defense of slavery."[49] Hence, while he became a southern slaveholder, Greene also succeeded in devising "a plan of admitting [his] negroes to the rights of copy holders," his ultimate goal being to "demolish slavery." [50] There is also some indication that Greene may have been attracted to deism in his last years of life. Though his correspondence with Thomas Paine and Thomas Jefferson, both of whom were deists, and John Witherspoon, his son's tutor, does not address his religious philosophy, it does refer to Greene's "agreeable" disposition towards the "voice of nature and reason." But effective proof of a deistic tendency stops here. What is more probable is that Greene continued to wrestle with his conflict of conviction.

Despite the fact that Nathanael Greene never renewed his membership in the Religious Society of Friends, he did achieve a partial reconciliation with that body through his treatment of Quakers in the last years of the Revolutionary War. Perhaps Greene never did learn to accept his role as a "Fighting Quaker," yet his example served to emphasize a fundamental contradiction in the Society's theology. Unknowingly, Greene was a victim of a contradiction which pitted the Quaker belief in pacifism against a more intrinsic belief in the doctrine of the Inner Light. To single out pacifism as the sole test of Quaker conviction, as many eighteenth-century Friends did, was to denigrate the very basis of Quaker thought itself, the Inner Light, which guides the individual in his search for religious and moral truth. Greene, then, like many Friends who joined the Continental Army, may very well have been following the leading of his Inner Light in his conviction as to the rightness of the Revolutionary cause. The Society of Friends' inability to recognize this contradiction, along with Greene's own economic interests and his devout patriotism, created a conflict of conviction for the Rhode Islander that plagued him throughout the Revolutionary period. What is most significant about Greene's example, though, is that by challenging the Society's discipline, the Rhode Island general paved the way for those patriotic Friends who served in the Civil War as well as in World Wars I and II, by demonstrating that a *Fighting* Quaker can also be a *Religious* one.

Endnotes

1 General Schuyler to George Washington, April 5, 1780 in John C. Fitzpatrick, editor, The Writings of George Washington, 1745-1799 (39 vols., Wasington D.C., 1933), XVIII, 185; See also Major John Clark Jr., to Nathanael Greene, January 10, 1777[8] in Richard K. Showman, editor, The Papers of General Nathanael Greene, 1766-1779 (5 vols. Chapel Hill, 1976) II, 249-50. Clark writes that "in case of an accident happening to General Washington [Greene] would be the properest person to command the army and that General Washington thought so too."

2 See Jack D. Marietta, The Reformation of American Quakerism, 1748-1783 (Philadelphia, 1984).

3 Edward Field, State of Rhode Island and Providence Plantations at the End of the Century (2 vols., Providence, 1902), II, 112; See also Rufus Jones, The Quakers in the American Colonies (London, 1911, 23-25. According to Jones, William Coddington and John Clarke, the founders of Portsmouth, united their town with the founders of Newport in 1641. Subsequently, the residents of Newport "arranged themselves into two religious groups." One of these groups held views which seemed "extraordinarily akin to those later held by the Society of Friends" while the other group formed a Baptist church. The former body met in a meetinghouse where "members spoke as they felt moved exactly as the Quaker meeting was held a little later." Consequently, 16 years before the arrival of the WoodHouse, which brought the first Quakers to Rhode Island, in 1657, there appears to have existed, in Newport, a group of people who were Quakers in everything but name. By 1660 the Friends had increased their numbers and held political posts in the Rhode Island Assembly. Despite the attempt of the Commissioners of the United Colonies to banish the Quakers from Rhode Island, the colony's assembly refused to comply, maintaining that "we have no law among us whereby to punish any for only declaring by words their minds and understandings concerning the ways of God." While Quakers continued to prosper in the Rhode Island colony, the records of the Massachusetts General Court show that they suffered persecution in that New England colony when they tried to spread their religious views. Perhaps the most noted of these Rhode Island Friends was Mary Dyer of Newport who was hanged on Boston Common, June 1, 1660.

4 Thyra Foster, "The Religious Society of Friends in Rhode Island, 1775-90" in Rhode Island Quakers in the American Revolution, 1775-1790 (Providence, 1976), 12-13.

5 Arthur J. Worral, Quakers in the Colonial Northeast (Hanover, N. H., 1980), 89, 99, 101-103.

6 See William G. McLoughlin, Rhode Island (New York, 1978), 74; McLoughlin claims that by 1739 thirty-six churches and one synagogue, representing six denominations existed in Rhode Island. This at a time when

most other colonies were trying to sustain conformity to one established church supported by religious taxes. Those churches in Rhode Island included: 12 Baptist churches, 10 Quaker meetinghouses, 6 Congregationalist churches, 5 Anglican churches, 1 Moravian church and 1 Jewish synagogue.

7 Ibid., 72-74.

8 Worral, Quakers in Northeast, 85.

9 Ibid., 82. The Religious Society of Friends organized a system of meetings that consisted of five levels. At the lowest level was the preparative meeting which is best described as an individual congregation and was most often referred to as a "meeting." One or more meetings made up the monthly meeting or the fundamental unit of the organizational structure. The monthly meeting had the power to accept into membership or to disown members, to marry members, to own property and to discipline members. Two or more monthly meetings composed a Quarterly meeting which dealt with more complex doctrinal or administrative matters that could be addressed by the monthly meeting. Several Quarterly meetings composed a yearly meeting which was independent of all others; no yearly meeting could control the discipline or organization of another yearly meeting. The yearly meeting made the most important decisions on doctrine and discipline in all of its subordinate meetings. In late eighteenth-century Rhode Island there were 23 preparative meetings and 5 monthly meetings: Rhode Island, located in Newport; Greenwich; Smithfield; South Kingstown and Providence. All of these came under the jurisdiction of New England Yearly Meeting held at Newport.

10 Ibid., 88-89. According to Worral, younger Friends, in particular, were greatly affected by the tightening of discipline as a majority of the offenses were marriage-related such as marrying outside of the Society of Friends or bastardy.

11 Field, State of R.I., II, 112. Field records the decline in membership among Rhode Island Quakers. He claims that in 1772 there were approximately 2,000 members and by 1813 the number had been reduced to 1,150.

12 Theodore Thayer, Nathanael Greene, Strategist of the American Revolution (New York, 1960), 18.

13 See Louise B. Clarke, The Greenes of Rhode Island with Historical Records of English Ancestry, 1534-1902 (2 vols., New York, 1903), I, 200-201. Nathanael Sr.'s father Jabez was also a Quaker and, according to Clarke, held a weekly meeting for worship at his house at Potowomut beginning in 1699. Jabez Greene inherited a forge at Potowomut from his father, James, an English immigrant. Jabez Greene ran the forge with his six sons and, thus, began the family business.

14 Ibid.

15 George Washington Greene, The Life of Nathanael Greene (3 vols., New York, 1871), I, 3-5.

16 Thayer, Strategist, 20-21.
17 Greene to Samuel Ward Jr., September 1771 in Showman, ed., Papers, I , 23-25.
18 Greene to Ward, September 1770 in ibid., 14-18.
19 Greene to Ward, August 29, 1772 in ibid., 38-46.
20 Greene to Ward, October 9, 1772 in ibid., 46-48.
21 See McLoughlin, Rhode Island, 81-82. In the mid-1750s two political factions had arisen in Rhode Island. These factions engaged in bitter fights to gain control of the colony's legislature. Samuel Ward, a wealthy Quaker merchant, led one faction which was centered in the southern part of Rhode Island and attracted mostly Anglicans and Quakers and was sympathetic to the needs of the Newport merchants. Stephen Hopkins, who would later become governor, led another faction which was centered in the northern part of the colony. The Hopkins faction attracted mostly Baptists and Congregationalists and was sympathetic to the rising merchants of Providence. Although neither party had a well-defined platform, they both sought to alleviate the burden of taxes and paper money redemption for their own particular supporters by placing most of it on their opposition. McLoughlin attributes the divisiveness of this Ward-Hopkins era, in part, to the growing conflict of interest between Rhode Island's commercial needs and those of the crown. While the Board of Trade wanted a stable hard-money system favorable to English creditors, Rhode Island wanted freedom in financial affairs, especially in trade. Hence, the Revolutionary War united both factions against the British trade policies.
22 See Arthur J. Mekeel, The Relation of the Quakers to the American Revolution (Washington D.C., 1979), 217-222. In 1742 at the time of King George's war, a militia act was passed in Rhode Island with a provision that "all persons making solemn engagement before the governor . . . that in time of war it is against their conscience to bear arms shall . . . be employed as scouts, messengers, watches or [serve] to remove women and children or sick persons out of immediate danger . . . and to do any other duty consistent with their religious principles." This clause, on indirect service, was contained in all of the subsequent militia acts of the Rhode Island colony including the Revolutionary War.
23 Records of the State of Rhode Island, VIII, 204.
24 See MS Minutes of New England Yearly Meeting for Sufferings, I , 60-61 at Moses Brown School, Providence Rhode Island.
25 See "Document, Nathanael Greene, Jacob Greene, Nathanael Greene Jr., and Eber Sweet" December 23, 1776 in Showman, Papers, I , 3-4.
26 Greene to Ward, April ?, 1772 in ibid., 26-31. According to editor Richard Showman, Dudingston's actions were attacked by the Newport Mercury which reported that "the piratical schooner belongs to King George III" and "we should think it below His Br-t-n-c Majesty to keep men-of-war employed in robbing some of his poorest subjects." The Rhode Island merchants threatened to "fit and arm a vessel to prevent any more seizures." On June 9, 1772 a party from Providence rowed towards the Gaspee, which

had run aground off Namquit Point, Warwick. They attacked the crew and set the ship on fire. Dudingston escaped with injuries.

[27] Greene to Ward, January 25, 1773 in ibid., 51-55.

[28] Oscar & Lillian Handlin, Liberty and Power, 1600-1760 (New York, 1986), 10-11. The Handlins claim that the term "right" assumed two distinctly different meanings during the seventeenth century. Until the mid-1770s the term was used to mean "property" or "possession." As the Revolution unfolded, though, the term adopted the Lockean definition as a quality inherent in men; a people's right against enslavement. Regardless, Greene believed that his rights, inalienable or economic, were exploited by the events of 1772.

[29] Greene to Ward, January 25, 1773 in Showman, Papers, I, 51-55.

[30] Greene to Ward, July 10, 1774 in ibid., 64-66.

[31] See "Subscription" August 29, 1774 in ibid., 67; and "Act Establishing the Kentish Guards" October 29, 1774 in ibid., 73-75.

[32] See "Appointment as Brigadier General of the Rhode Island Army" May 1775 in ibid., 78-79.

[33] Greene to wife Catharine, June 2, 1775 in ibid., 82-83; See also John & Janet Stegeman, Caty, A Biography of Catharine Littlefield Greene (Providence, 1977), 49-50. Ironically, Catharine Greene's indifference to any religion, let alone Quakerism, must have given her husband some consolation as his decision to go to war had very little impact on her in a religious sense. More interesting is the the response of Greene's mother, Mary Mott Greene. When this staunch Quaker woman learned of her son's desire to go to war she supposedly told him: "Well Nathanael, if thee must engage in this carnal warfare in defence of thy country, never let me hear of thee being wounded with thy back to the enemy."

[34] See William Johnson, ed., Sketches of the Life and Correspondence of Nathanael Greene (2 vols., New York, 1930), II, 451.

[35] Greene to Governor Nicholas Cook of Rhode Island, December 21, 1776 in Showman, Papers, I, 374-76; and Greene to Christopher Greene, January 20, 1777 in ibid., II, 9.

[36] See Mekeel, Relation of Quakers, 173-84. Mekeel points out that the public, as well as the Continental Army, could not understand the absolutist position of the Friends in refusing to contribute to the war effort in any way. Considering the pressures of war and the struggle for national survival, the Friends with their neutral position instigated the public accusations of toryism. In southeastern Pennsylvania, a center of Quakerism, these allegiances were most severe. In fact some of the more prominent Philadelphia Friends were sent into exile to Virginia by the Congress, in 1778; this due to a widespread suspicion of their aid to General Howe's army.

[37] Greene to wife, Catharine, September 14, 1777 in Showman, Papers, II, 163.

[38] See Greene to Jacob Greene, June 4, 1777; Greene to Jacob Greene, October 27, 1777; and Greene to Miss Susan Livingston, November 11, 1777; in ibid.

[39] Religious Society of Friends, East Greenwich Monthly Meeting Minutes: 4 mo./5/1777; See also Greene to Jacob Greene, June 4, 1777 in Showman, Papers, II, 142. The Miunites of the East Greenwich Monthly Meeting of August 1773 record that Nathanael Greene had participated in a military gathering at Plainfield Connecticut, just over the Rhode Island border. The Meeting appointed three Friends to vist him and solicit a promise for behavior in accord with the pacifist principles of the Society of Friends. Greene refused to make such a promise and was suspended -- not expelled -- from membership. He remained on the meeting's membership rolls, however, until April 5, 1777 when he formally requested to be dropped from the care of the Meeting. Had Greene been a member of one of the Philadelphia-area meetings, he most likely would have been disowned after his refusal to adopt a pacifist stance. The New England Meetings were much more lenient with their membership since its members were largely indigenous in origin and came to the Society from Quaker missionary activities rather than as immigrants from England with the background of religious persecution that motivated settlement in America. Not surprisingly, the New England meetings made an effort to cooperate with their colonial assemblies throughout the war and were extremely careful in their handling of those members who went to war.

[40] See John B. Trussell, Jr., Birthplace of an Army, A Study of the Valley Forge Encampment (Harrisburg, Pa., 1979), 13. The British had established winter quarters in the city of Philadelphia, eighteen miles southeast of Valley Forge, a position which presented a constant specter of invasion and one which prevented the Continental Army from securing supplies through the port of Philadelphia. Additionally, many of the inhabitants in the area of the encampment were Quaker farmers who were averse to provisioning the army due to their pacifist convictions.

[41] Greene to Reverend Jihn Murray, January ?, 1778, in Showman, Papers, 263.

[42] Trussell, Birthplace, 82; See also Donald B. Chidsey, Valley Forge (New York, 1966), 79-80.

[43] Reverend John Murray to Greene, January 21, 1780, in Showman, Papers, V, 298-300.

[44] Letter of William DeWees, February, 1778, in Mrs. Philip E. La Monyan, ed., The DeWees Family Papers (Valley Forge, Pa., 1902), 18; See also "Account of Mary Thomas Jones," March 10, 1829 in Priscilla Walker Streets, ed., Lewis Walker of Chester Valley (Philadelphia, 1896), 76.

[45] Greene to George Washington, January 1778, in Showman, Papers, II, 262-66. In his letter to Washington Greene makes a plea on behalf of all the officers, for a pension of half-pay for life. Although he clearly identifies

this motive, his language, again, illustrates the conflict of conviction apparent in his earlier writings. One must question where his loyalties now rest; with political allegiance or with a more personal interest.

[46] Greene to the Members of New Garden Monthly Meeting near Guilford Court House, March 26, 1781; and New Garden Monthly Meeting to Greene, March 30, 1781 in American Friend, II , (1895): 307.

[47] Abel James & Thomas Winslow to Greene, June 4, 1781; and Greene to Abel James & Thomas Winslow, June 7, 1781, Perkins Library, Duke University.

[48] Letter of Edward Stabler, December 19, 1781, Cox, Wharton & Parrish Collection, Historical Society of Pennsylvania.

[49] Greene quoted in George Washington Greene, Life of Greene, III, 519. When Greene was attacked by a Quaker for holding slaves, the Rhode Islander tried to explain his position by alluding to the nature of the time period: "As for slavery, nothing can be said in its defense. But you are much mistaken respecting my influence in this business. With all the address I was master of, I could not obtain the liberty of a small number even for the defense of the country and though the necessity stood confessed, yet the motion was rejected. The generosity of the southern states has placed an interest of this sort [i.e., plantations cultivated by slave labor] in my hands and I trust their condition will not be worse but better."

[50] Dr. Gordon to Greene, September 26, 1785 in ibid., 519-20.

Thomas Paine, author of "Common Sense"
from an engraving by W. Sharp
(Courtesy of the New York Historical Society, New York City)

Title Page of Thomas Paine's "Common Sense" (1776)
(Courtesy of the American Philosophical Society)

Nathanael Greene by Charles W. Peale
(Courtesy of Independence National Historical Park)

" 'Mad Anthony' Wayne Refusing the Offer of a Blanket from a Woman Patriot at Valley Forge"

From a Painting by D.A. Sullard. Photograh by Will Brown
(Courtesy of the Dietrich American Collection)

**Valley Friends Meeting House
& School House
(Society of Friends)**
Artist's Conception by Mary Jane Walker, 1937
(Courtesy of Friends Historical Library, Swarthmore College)

61

From the Monthly Meeting of FRIENDS,

Called by Some

The FREE QUAKERS,

Held by Adjournment at Philadelphia, on the 9th Day of the 7th Month, 1781.

To those of our Brethren who have disowned us.

BRETHREN,

AMONG the very great number of persons whom you have disowned for matters religious and civil, a number have felt a necessity of uniting together for the discharge of those religious duties, which we undoubtedly owe to God and to one another. We have accordingly met and having seriously considered our situation, agreed to establish and endeavour to support, on the ancient and sure foundation, meetings for public worship, and meetings for conducting our religious affairs. And we rejoice in a firm hope, that as we humble ourselves before God, his presence will be found in them, and his blessing descend and rest upon them.

As you have by your proceedings against us separated yourselves from us, and declared that you have no unity with us, you have compelled us, however unwillingly, to become separate from you. And we are free to declare to you and to the world, that we are not desirous of having any mistake which we may happen to make laid to your charge; neither are we willing to have any of your errors brought as guilt against us. To avoid these, seeing that you have made the separation, we submit to have a plain line of distinction drawn between us and you. But there are some points which seem to require a comparison of sentiment between you and us, and some kind of decision to be made upon them. The property of that society of which we and you were once joint members, is far from being inconsiderable, and we have done nothing which can afford even a pretension of our having forfeited our right therein.

Whether you have or have not a right to declare to the world your sentiments of the conduct of any individual: Or whether you have or have not a right to sit in judgment over and pass sentence upon your christian brethren differing in sentiment from you, although educated among you, are not questions now to be considered: But you having taken upon you to do those things, it remains only to be enquired, What are the consequences in law and equity of your having so done. Surely you will not pretend that *our right* is destroyed by those *acts of yours*. But we suggest to your consideration, Whether your conduct has or has not in law, disqualified you to hold any part of that property? A serious and full consideration of this question, and the critical and strikingly singular situation in which you stand, cannot injure you; but it may, possibly, induce you to consider, with the more candour and readiness, what equity requires to be done by you toward us, or by us toward you. And tend to a decision the most proper between brethren, differing in sentiment one from another concerning their respective rights to property, yet each believing in him whose precepts leads us to "do unto others as we would they should do unto us."

Whatever may have been the consequences to yourselves, either of your conduct toward us as friends to the present revolution; or of your conduct in other cases, less immediately respecting us, it seems to be unquestionably certain, that we have not done any thing which can possibly forfeit *our right*. And we see no reason why we should surrender it up to you; but think it a duty incumbent on us to assert our claim.

As a place for holding our meetings for worship, and meetings for business relative to the society is become necessary for us, since you have separated yourselves from us, by testifying against us, and thereby rendering it highly improper for us to appear among you, as one people, at your meetings, we think it proper for us to use, apart from you, one of the houses built by friends in this city for those purposes. We are desirous of doing this in the most decent and unexceptionable manner, and are willing to hear any thing which you may chuse to say on the subject: And, therefore, we thus invite you to the opportunity of doing it, and of shewing what degree of kindness and brotherly love toward us, still remains among you. We also mean to use the burial ground, whenever the occasion shall require it: For, however the living may contend, surely the dead may lie peaceably together.

Lest any may infer too much from this representation, we think it proper explicitly to declare, that should our right to the property in question be found, in the law, to be superior to yours, from any consideration whatever, it is far, very far from our wish to seclude you from a joint participation with us in the use of it: Neither do we mean to solicit a decision in law, unless you by your conduct compel us to it.

We sincerely and earnestly desire to have this subject amicably, equitably and speedily adjusted, and request that this free communication of our sentiments may be made known to all who are usually consulted on business among you, and that, for this purpose, it may be read when you next meet together on religious business.

As Christians, labouring in some degree to forgive injuries, we salute you, and, though disowned and rejected by you, we are your friends and brethren.

Signed in, and on behalf of the said Meeting, by

SAMUEL WETHERILL, jun. CLERK.

The First Broadside Issued by the Free Quaker Society (1781)
(Courtesy of the Friends Historical Library, Swarthmore College)

**Free Quaker Timothy Matlack
by Charles W. Peale**
(Courtesy of Independence National Historical Park)

Free Quaker Meeting House 1783
5th and Arch Streets, Philadelphia, Pennsylvania

The Free Quaker Meeting House (1783)
5th & Arch Streets, Philadelphia, Pennsylvania
Sketch by Fletcher MacNeill, 1968
(Courtesy of the Free Quaker Society)

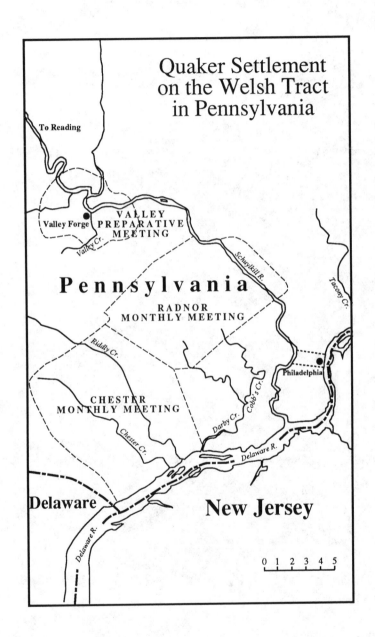

Quaker Settlement
on the Welsh Tract
in Pennsylvania

To Reading

Valley Forge

VALLEY
PREPARATIVE
MEETING

Valley Cr.

Schuylkill R.

Pennsylvania

RADNOR
MONTHLY MEETING

Tacony Cr.

Riddly Cr.

Philadelphia

CHESTER
MONTHLY MEETING

Cobb's Cr.

Darby Cr.

Chester Cr.

Delaware R.

Delaware

New Jersey

Delaware R.

0 1 2 3 4 5

Chapter 3

Quakerism, Patriotism & Transformation in the Valley Forge Community, 1684 - 1778

The Continental Army's encampment at Valley Forge, Pennsylvania, during the winter of 1777 - 1778 has provided ample subject matter for generations of popular historians. [1] The mythology surrounding the encampment has been offset by some of the more recent scholarship on the American Revolution. [2] While most of these works emphasize the military and political aspects of the encampment period, the research of Jack Marietta, Barry Levy and Wayne Bodle has been particularly helpful in understanding the demographic history of the Valley Forge area and its impact on the Army's stay there. [3]

The relationship of the Valley Forge area residents to the Continental Army is significant in understanding both the extent to which the Revolutionary movement was dependent upon the compliance of the American people and the receptivity of those people to the cause of independent from Great Britain. To be certain, Valley Forge, and the Army's survival under adverse living conditions during the winter of 1777-78, served as a turning point in the War of Independence and thus provides a useful source for study.[4]

This chapter will demonstrate that there was a broad spectrum of compliance and non-compliance to the war effort among the Quaker farmers of the Valley Forge area. [5] This mixed reception to the needs of the Army can be attributed to the gradual deterioration of Quaker values within the community long before Washington's troops arrived there. Over the course of forty years prior to the winter encampment of 1777-78, Valley Forge had been transformed from a homogeneous, agrarian community of devout Welsh Quakers to a more heterogeneous, capitalist-oriented society of many religious denomination, and one which was more receptive to the political concerns that would provoke the American Revolution. Regardless of their choice to promote, discourage or ignore the American course, the lives of the Valley Forge Friends were deeply affected by their cause of action. Consequently, the suffering experienced at Valley Forge, during the winter encampment of 1777-78 was not confined to the officers and men of the Continental Army, rather it was a mutual sufferance of citizenry and soldiery alike.

Valley Forge established its roots in the Quaker settlement of Pennsylvania. As early as 1684 William Penn provided for "about forty thousand acres" which " may be lay'd out contiguously as one Barony" for the purpose of Welsh settlement. [6] An adjacent parcel of 7,800 acres was retained by Penn and granted to his daughter, Letitia, as a provincial manor, this land would later comprise the encampment area. [7]

Known as the "Welsh Tract," this fertile Great Valley of Chester and northwestern Philadelphia counties was blessed with rolling hills and a network of creeks which emptied into a main tributary, the Schuylkill river. Penn granted this land to seven companies which were to subdivide the territory among its members, Quakers, primarily from the counties of Merionethshire and Radnorshire, Wales. [8] Free of the religious persecution and devastating economic circumstances of the Old World, [9] these first purchasers hoped to establish an independent, Quaker community "within which all causes, quarrels, crimes and disputes might be wholly determined by people of "their own language."[10] Familial relations were also instrumental in their decision to immigrate to Pennsylvania.

The financial constraints of the Welsh Quakers compelled some to place their children in the service of another, more affluent individual. Other children simply left their parents' farmlands, when they came of age, for the better economic prospects of the city. Combined with persecutions and heavy fines for practicing their religious convictions, these poor economic conditions and the concomitant breaking up of the family unit made it very difficult for Welsh Friends to raise their children in an atmosphere of "Holy Conversation" or behavior that was conducive to securing the child's salvation.[11] Friends believed that their children were born with both original sin and Christ's redeeming seed. The environment in which their children were raised and the strength of their character as parents would determine which one --sin or seed -- would take precedent in the child's life. [12] Not surprisingly, many of these Welsh Quakers were eager to accept Penn's offer when he promoted his New World colony as the place to save Quaker familialism. Penn promised contiguous holdings of 100 to 500 acres apiece to each farmer who settled in his colony, claiming that cheap land would permit a "more convenient bringing up of youth" and end the need to "put their children into another Gentleman's service". [13]

Barry Levy in his work, Quakers and the American Family, discovered the connection between Quaker domesticity and economic prosperity in the quest of these Welsh Friends to secure an environment conducive to holy conversation for their children. Levy argues that "for Quaker parents establishing 'holy conversation' meant establishing their children on decently wealthy farms, married to Friends of their own choosing but with parental approval." [14] Accordingly, the Quaker immigrants who settled on the Welsh Tract accumulated vast amounts of land so they could distribute them among their children, keeping them close to home. Levy found that by the late 1690s the mean holding of the seventy resident families on the Welsh Tract was 322 acres. [15] These Friends continued to purchase land after 1700 to give to their children, the operating belief being that "three hundred acres would seem to insure a new household's protection from the world." [16]

In their quest for a Quaker utopia the Welsh Friends also depended on the monthly meeting. The role of this institution was to nurture the religious life of its membership by providing for an education, regulating marriages, communicating with other, more distant, meetings and their members, disciplining anyone guilty of a moral offense and controlling the funds of its congregation. Essentially, the monthly meeting dominated each aspect of each phase in the lives of its members. By the 1720s the activities of Friends in the Welsh Tract were rather closely monitored by the twelve monthly meetings that existed in the area. [17]

The local meetings encouraged their members to circulate within the confines of the Society of Friends, limiting their association with non-Quakers to less intimate dealings. Disownment, for example, became the punishment for marrying out of the faith. [18] Indentured servants, apprentices or anyone who entered the realm of the nuclear family was to be of the Quaker persuasion as the monthly meeting cautioned Friends to be "careful what persons they brought or admitted to their families." [19] Even those Philadelphia Quakers who removed to the Great Valley area had to submit proof of an "innocent and sober character" being a "diligent frequenter of Meetings" before their membership could be transferred.[20] The religiously-guarded education of youth was also a high priority of the Valley Friends. There existed at least three day schools, by 1720, operating under the care of the Friends for " one whole year" in length "except for two weeks" in order to accommodate the Yearly Meeting proceedings and harvest time. [21] In short, Quakerism in the Welsh Tract endured through the interaction of the family, the school and the meeting.

This early Quaker community was also a self-sustaining one based upon an agrarian economy. A visitor to the Welsh Tract, in 1708, claimed that the "inhabitants have many large plantations of corn and wheat" and "an abundance of cattle insomuch that they are looked upon to be in as thriving a condition as any place in the Province." [22] The observation gives testimony to the success of the Welsh settlers and their children, many of whom became involved in bi-occupationalism. Industries closely associated with farming such as flour milling and grist milling became common subsidiary enterprises in the lives of the second generation. Nor was it uncommon among the second generation to retain the services of white indentured servants. [23] To be certain, these Welsh Quakers, in just twenty years time, had achieved a utopian community based on holy conversation.

Beginning in the 1740s however, with the maturing of the third generation, the Welsh Tract witnessed a transformation, becoming a more heterogeneous and capitalist-oriented society. This transformation was affected by two phenomena: the Quaker adherence to a "Calvinistic-like" work ethic and the increased immigration of non-Welsh immigrants, notably the German Lutherans and the Scotch-Irish Presbyterians.

Although pious in their intent, the adherence of the second generation to the Protestant work ethic resulted in a concern for more worldly affairs among their children. The daily toil of the land was regarded by Quakers as a religious duty. While idleness among Friends was the "breeder of vice and vain conversation," the tilling of the soil inspired "true Godliness...enabling [men] to live better in the world." [24] Accordingly, the harder one worked the more devout he became in doing God's will and in creating a protective, religiously-guarded environment for his children. Concomitant to this work ethic was the financial success of individual enterprise; a success which allowed the second generation inhabitants of the Welsh Tract to become more affluent and, their children, more worldly than their forbearers.

Levy's examination of probate inventories of the Great Valley residents amply illustrates the increased material prosperity of Friends. Comparing the inventories of 80 Welsh Tract and Chester Quaker households before 1730 with those of 69 Welsh Tract and Chester Quaker households between 1731 and 1776, Levy found that Friends lived more simply before 1730. The households of the first generation had an average personal income of 192 pounds sterling. These Quaker settlers appear to have slept in nice beds, ate on pewter places and had an average of three chairs per household. However, they stored their possessions in trunks and boxes, rarely ate with knives and forks and few had extraneous furniture. Those inventories taken after 1730, however, reveal a very difficult lifestyle. The average personal income of the second generation was 331 pounds sterling. The children of the Quaker settlers also enjoyed many more luxuries than their parents for the first generation: 70% more rural households owned a chest-of-drawers, 30% more owned desks, 37% more owned clocks, 45% more owned large looking glasses, 20% more owned books, 24% more owned table linen and 33% more owned knives and forks. [25]

Personal wealth also increased after 1730 due to the growing industry of the Great Valley area. Although a crude Mount Joy forge existed as early as 1718, the local iron works industry was more fully established by the mid-eighteenth century. This "Valley Forge" as it was called, flourished with the arrival, in 1757, of a Quaker entrepreneur John Potts. By the mid-1760s Potts had added a grist mill and a shallow draft boat to his enterprise in order to broaden his market and cut his transportation costs, delivering his wares more easily by river to Reading and to Philadelphia rather than over land. [26] Potts was clearly the most prosperous Quaker in the Great Valley, his estate being worth 7,586 pounds sterling at his death in 1768. [27] The rise of freemen or financially independent bachelors over twenty-one years of age, after 1750, in the Great Valley is also indicative of the increase in personal wealth that came to the Welsh Tract. [28]

72

The economic emphasis, then, was no longer placed on securing a comfortable subsistence for one's family, but rather on a profit motive.

This changing influence and the capitalist-orientation it bred resulted in the deterioration of "holy conversation" among Friends of the Welsh Tract. No longer would property be accumulated and handed down to the next generation to the extent that the first Welsh settlers had planned, rather it would be sold off to those who could pay top price. Levy tells us that compared to their parents, the second generation gave much less land to their children. While the first settlers provided their children with an average of 701 acres, the second generation gave an average of 400 acres to theirs. Land distribution was also lower. Although the first generation was able to give 72% of their sons an average 278.3 acres, the second generation gave 64.7% of their sons an average of 151.2 acres. Most of the second generation's sons received less than 200 acres and over 60% got less than 100 acres or no land at all. [29] Hence, Quaker piety became the casualty of increasing commercialization in the Welsh Tract.

An increase in Scotch-Irish and German immigration also threatened the religiously-guarded community of the Welsh Tract during the 1740s and 1750s. To be certain, the Welsh Friends were forced to confront the threat of non-Quaker influence as early as 1707 when an Anglican missionary came to the Great Valley. Within five years time, the Reverend Evans had established a congregation "consisting for the most part of persons brought over from the Quakers." The English clergyman had eliminated the cultural barrier by "preaching in Welsh one fortnight for four years." [30] However, this early defection from the Society of Friends had a significant impact on the network of communication which developed among the Great Valley's Quakers, one which renewed their original intentions of developing a self-sustaining, religiously-guarded utopia. [31] Times had changes, though, and the capitalist-orientation of the second generation prompted them to employ non-Quaker servants.

By the 1740s, the most readily available labor force came from Scotland and Germany. [32] These immigrants worked along with other non-Quaker Welsh servants to cultivate the farmlands of the fertile Great Valley. Each brought along their own culture, which inevitably conflicted with that of the Welsh. The intermingling of the Scotch-Irish and Welsh Presbyterians, for example, produced arguments over the primacy of the English or Welsh language in the church service and over the educational criterion of their minister, a debate that reached the highest levels of Presbyterianism and served as a motivating force of the First Great Awakening. [33] The emotionalism of the Awakening itself, with its anti-establishment and secular tendencies had a mass appeal in the Great Valley. The itinerary Evangelists who carried the revivalist sentiment of the Awakening were "adored by the generality of [their] hearers" and became "greatly successful" in preach[ing] men out of reason," making them "raving mad." [34] In this way, the Great Awakening of the 1740s helped to make the various Protestant denominations of the Great Valley more tolerant, even respectful, of one another. In fact, by 1750, the Reverend Henry M. Mulenberg of the local German Lutheran Church recorded in his journal that he "preached an English sermon" to another local congregation and the people being "very attentive and much moved....desired that [he] should come frequently." [35]

Quaker dominance in the region, as well as the internal discipline of the Society, began to diminish with the greater influx of other religious and ethnic groups. The third generation, their parents having lowered the religiously-protective barriers, became attracted by the social and financial prosperity that interaction with the non-Friends of the Great Valley promised to bring. Disownment for marrying out of the meeting became a common occurrence among Friends of the third generation, [36] while negligence in abiding by the meeting discipline was manifested in their "use and distilling of Spirituous liquors" and even the "purchasing and keeping of negro slaves." [37] More sensational, was the increased incidence of fornication among third generation Friends, which doubled in Chester county after the 1740s. [38] Jack Marietta in his brilliant work, The Reformation of American Quakerism, 1748 - 1783, found that the " miseducation of Quaker children, irregular marriages and the liberal admission of offspring [into the Society of Friends] together had produced a mottled generation, hardly able or willing to cure itself." [39] Only the second generation could be blamed for this set of circumstances. While many of these Friends may have believed that Quaker doctrine demanded that their children be guided -- not coerced -- into the tenets of their faith, it had become apparent, by 1755, that "truth was at a low ebb" in the Welsh Tract, "especially amongst elders and those of advanced years." [40] Marietta claims that this dilution of Quaker piety and the refusal of third generation Friends to adhere to the discipline of the Society provoked a spiritual reformation among the Pennsylvania Quakers. This reformation began with the visit of an English Quaker minister, Samuel Fothergill, on the eve of the French-Indian War and continued throughout the eighteenth century. [41]

Fothergill visited every monthly and quarterly meeting during his visit to Pennsylvania, in addition to meetings for worship and Quaker families. He reprimanded Friends for the "weak and almost ruined state of our discipline" and encouraged them to withdraw from the larger society and their worldly concerns in order to concentrate on the purification of the Society as a religious body. Near the end of his stay, Fothergill delivered his famous excoriation of Pennsylvania Friends; a statement which aptly characterizes the circumstances that had transpired among the Quakers of the Welsh Tract:

> Their fathers came into the country in its
> infancy and bought large tracts of land for
> a trifle; their sons found large estates
> come into their possession and a

profession of religion which was partly national, which descended like the patrimony from their fathers, and cost as little. They settled in ease and affluence and whilst they made the barren wilderness as a fruitful field, suffered the plantation of God to be as a field uncultivated and a desert. Thus, decay of discipline and other weakening things prevailed to the eclipsing of Zion's beauty;... A people who had thus beat their swords into plowshares and the bent of their spirits to this world could not instruct their offspring in those statutes they had themselves forgotten. As every like begets its like, a generation was likely to succeed, formed upon other maxims, if the everlasting Father had not mercifully extended a visitation to supply the deficiency of their natural parents. [42]

Despite the attempts of Fothergill and other American Quaker reformers to tighten meeting discipline and reorganize the meeting structure to make Friends accountable for their behavior, [43] the spiritual reformation could not "save" all of the third generation Friends. This fact would become apparent during the outbreak of hostilities between the colonies and Great Britain when some of the Great Valley's most prominent Quakers defied the Society's Peace Testimony in order to serve the colony in a political or military capacity. [44]

During the course of nearly a century, the intensive cultivation of the "inward plantation" (i.e. religious life) had come under increasing pressure due to the concerns of the "outward plantation" (i.e. the material world). [45] The Great Valley had become a fairly permissive society in which it was easy for Quakers to deviate from meeting discipline. Consequently, by the time of the American Revolution, third generation Friends had lost the consensus of "holy conversation" so carefully nurtured by their Welsh forefathers and began to pursue a variety of lifestyles. To be sure, there were those third

76

generation Friends in the Great Valley, the majority, who adhered to the directives of the Society, leading a religiously-guarded life. By doing so, these Quakers remained true to the ideals of Fothergill's spiritual reformation. However, there existed another segment of the Great Valley's Quaker population which ignored the exhortations of the spiritual reformers and pursued a course of wealth and non-Quaker ways. These Friends, in particular, had a vested interest in the capitalist values of the Revolutionary movement. For them, a secure economic existence based on a productive agrarian life was fundamental to the yeoman's idea of the "pursuit of happiness," whether he was an industrial entrepreneur or a commercial farmer. There was still another group of Friends in the Great Valley who were caught between the values of their pious and worldly brethren. These Quakers were uncertain of their commitment to pacifism, on the one hand, and to a capitalist-oriented patriotism, on the other. This group would incur the greatest suffering during the Revolutionary War. These, then, were the range of sentiments held by the Quaker inhabitants of the Valley Forge community, attitudes to which the Continental Army would be exposed during the winter encampment, December 19, 1777 to June 19, 1778.

A Mutual Sufferance: Citizenry, Soldiery & Necessity during the Valley Forge Encampment, 1777-1778

General George Washington's decision to establish winter quarters at Valley Forge was based on a number of considerations. Foremost among these was the terrain of the area. Bounded by high grounds and waterways, the territory provided an excellent means for fortification and defense in case of an attack. [46] Conversely, Valley Forge, though remote from most settled areas, was only eighteen miles northwest of British-occupied Philadelphia, enabling Washington to maintain some degree of intelligence on the activities of General Howe and his forces. [47] The provisioning of the army was also an important factor in Washington's decision and one which would inevitably involve the Quaker population of the Valley Forge area.

Late in the 1777 campaign, the Continental Army's reserves of bread and meat were sparse. [48] Accordingly, the army's diet was increasingly supplemented by "fire-cake"; a thin bread made of flour and water baked over a camp fire. If additional food stores were to be secured the army would be compelled to forage the countryside, as the inefficiency of the military supply departments and the inability of Congress to procure provisions had rendered Washington and his troops helpless. [49]

Additional provisioning might be obtained by access to the rich farmlands of Chester county, the best remaining local source of food and grain. Yet by December 23, 1777, four days after the army's arrival at Valley Forge, Washington wrote that his army "must inevitably starve, dissolve or disperse in order to obtain subsistence in the best manner they can." [50] The Commander's prediction appeared to be coming true by February, 1778 as many troops were "destitute of meat," and even worse, desertions were astonishingly great. [51]

78

The non-compliance of many local inhabitants can be identified as a cause for the military sufferance. The pacifist convictions of many local Quakers dictated their actions toward the army. Strict adherents to the peace testimony, these Friends believed that aid to the soldiers in even the most indirect ways -- serving as hospital attendants, accepting Continental promissory notes for grain, lending their horses for the army's use or taking an oath of allegiance [52] -- constituted an infringement of their religious discipline and was, therefore, a cause for disownment from the Society of Friends. [53] However, not all those who refused to comply were, like the Quakers, conscientious objectors. Many were Baptists, Lutherans and Presbyterians who were strapped by economic considerations. These were "poor labouring men having little or no other subsistence but what they earned by their daily labour." For them, support of the army, in any form, constituted a "heavy and oppressive grievance." [54]

There were also those inhabitants who did comply, albeit to varying degrees, in fulfilling the needs of the Continental Army. Provisioning of the army in order to "relieve half clad and shivering soldiers as well as private individuals" took many forms. The quartering of officers in private residences along the encampment boundaries was one method of alleviating the military sufferance. [55] Ironically, the few loyalists in the vicinity of Valley Forge forfeited their properties for this purpose when they left the area to "join the enemy in Philadelphia." [56] Prominent Anglican William Moore of Moore Hall, one of the loyalists who did remain in the area, buckled under the increased pressure of the Revolutionary movement. Moore, who had "no faith in the [American] rabble," was coerced into housing the Committee of Correspondence when it visited the encampment in 1778. [57]

Another means of compliance, and one more amenable to the pacifist Quakers, was caring for the sick. To this end, the local Valley Friends meetinghouse became a military hospital and the adjoining graveyard a burial ground for the army's casualties. [58] Still another means of support was supplying the Continentals with grain and food stores. There were even those inhabitants who "baked for the soldiers and furnished them with a pound of bread for a pound of flour." [59] At the other extreme were those local residents who were apolitical. Their support of the Continental army or even the British army depended on their own economic prosperity. These individuals only dealt with Washington's troops when paid in specie for their goods and they demanded exorbitant prices for their items. Trade with the British in Philadelphia was preferred only because Commanding officer William Howe could afford to pay these profiteers more readily with hard coin. [60]

The most patriotic group of supporters, however, were those who "left their ploughs and assumed the military garb." [61] Most of these individuals belonged to the Great Valley Baptist Church, having been inspired by their fiery pastor, David Jones. [62] The Baptist preacher received his appointment in the Continental Army in April 1776 and served as Brigade Chaplain for the Pennsylvania troops. [63] The Presbyterians and Anglicans of the Great Valley volunteered for military services to a lesser degree but among their numbers were some of the most prominent personalities of the Revolution. Leading the list was Brigadier General Anthony Wayne, commanding officer of the Pennsylvania line, and Captains Henry Pawling and John Davis. [64] There were even those Quakers who ignored the pacifist directives of their meeting to join the military service. Among these were John Moore and William DeWees, both of whom were officers in the Pennsylvania militia. [65] These local officers served to inspire their neighbors as several "male inhabitants fit to [serve] had deserted their dwellings" in order to "take up arms against [the British]." [66]

The diversity of treatment by the civilian population elicited an equally diverse response from the Continental Army. Initially, fairness dictated the military's actions. An attempt was made to compensate the inhabitants for their inconvenience. For example, whenever private dwellings were requisitioned for use as officer's quarters the residents were paid rent or provided with protection against the capricious element of the Army. Promissory notes were given to those who supplied the Continentals with food stores. [67] Similarly Washington opened a camp market to provide local farmers with some income as well as an alternative to profiteering. [68] Still when the vital interests of the rebel army required civilian exploitation, the soldiers did not hesitate to plunder the properties of the inhabitants.

The incidence of depredation at the hands of the Continental Army were greatest during two different periods of the six-month encampment: 1) late December 1777 into the early part of January 1778; and 2) the middle weeks of February 1778. During these periods famine reached epidemic proportions as even fire-cake was lacking. One farmer complained that his "winter crop [was] entirely ruined, [his] meadow left without any fence" and that the soldiers made "a common practice of taking [his] horses." Others were stopped by "half-uniformed soldiers" on the roads leading to the city, their produce "being seized by these highway robber." [69] Brigadier General James Varnum articulated the circumstances of the army most succinctly when, in February, he wrote: The love of freedom which once animated the breast of those born in the country is controlling by hunger, the keenest of necessities." [70]

Seizure of civilian property was not limited to food stores either. The need for hospitals compelled the physicians of the Continental Army to commandeer some of the local churches for that purpose. "Forcible entry" was made into the "meetinghouse and stable" of one local Quaker meeting despite the protestations of the caretaker. Similarly, a "spiteful commissary and a surgeon of the American Army ... took over St. Peter's [Lutheran] church for hospital use" and "had even filled the parsonage with sick soldiers." [71]

This adverse treatment of the citizenry by the Continental Army resulted in a wide-spread sufferance, intimately affecting the lives of the local inhabitants. [72] Destruction of property was the most common of the depredations, as unruly soldiers plundered homesteads "for three miles in every direction" of the encampment. Damages of individual estates ranged from the "breaking of furniture and other [household] items" to the complete destruction of dwellings. [73] The DeWees family's loss, totaling 4,171 pounds currency, was the greatest in the area as the local ironworks industry and the two outbuildings including the family home, were destroyed by both the British and American armies. [74]

The religious lives of the inhabitants were also disrupted by the debacle of the Continental Army. Local Quakers were not only forbidden to attend their yearly meeting in Philadelphia, as such travel constituted a threat to rebel intelligence, but were limited in their visitation to other monthly and quarterly meetings in Chester County as well. In fact few Friends were able to attend the weekly meeting for worship, "owing to the present commotions." [75] Irregularity in the proceedings of the vestrymen demonstrated that the nearby Presbyterian and Anglican churches were also plagued by this inconvenience. [76]

More significant though, were the divisions of families and neighbors as a result of differing loyalties. Anglican preacher William Currie had reared three sons, all of whom entered the American army at the outbreak of hostilities. His political differences with them and his poor health left him near destitute in old age. [77] Familial conflict also prevailed among the Quakers. The record books of the local meetings were riddled with disownments of those who had "deviated from the peaceable principles of Friends" for any number of reasons; not necessarily for direct military participation. [78] This inconsistency in the position of the local Quakers earned, for them, the great suspicion of their neighbors too.

Frequently, Friends were assumed to be of the loyalist persuasion. Widespread rumors of their voluntary aid to the British cause provoked the wrath of their more patriotic acquaintances. [79] Accordingly, the provincial government, the military and local officials took indiscriminate, albeit precautionary, action against the Great Valley Quakers. These actions included the seizure of personal property, the imposition of fines and even imprisonment. [80]

This wide scale of treatment and suffering experienced by the citizenry at the hands of the Continental Army and the diverse receptivity of the army by the local population brings into question the fundamental purpose of the Revolutionary movement. Was independence from Great Britain, in fact, a popular cause or simply the desire of a small coterie of politically-motivated individuals? The attitudes of the soldiery and citizenry of Valley Forge indicate that it was neither. Both parties had simply been caught in the cross-fire of the Revolutionary movement, being forced to confront the contradictions which unfolded during the winter of 1777 - 1778.

Two generations had passed since the arrival of the Quakers in the Valley Forge area. The socioeconomic transformation of their community made many third generation Friends more worldly, more accepting of non-Quaker lifestyles. To be certain, a Quaker industrialist like Isaac Potts or William Dewees, the owners of the local ironworks, maintained a vested interest in the Revolution because of the increased income it afforded them in supplying the army equipment. Even less prosperous Friends engaged in commercial farming were attracted to the promise of greater economic prosperity that an independent America might bring; this was fundamental to the yeoman's idea of the "pursuit of happiness." However, these sentiments presented the ultimate challenge to Quaker religiosity because the means of attaining economic prosperity required support for a military effort.

83

While the majority of the Valley Friends had become engaged by the spiritual reformation that was taking place within the Society and adhered to the pacifist directives of their meetings, there were those who did "turn out in defense of their country." [81] These Fighting Friends were influenced by the pro-Revolutionary sentiments of their neighbors, particularly the intensely-patriotic Baptists, who believed that "a defensive war" for their liberties and properties "was sinless before God" and "to engage therein [was] consistent with the purest religion." [82]

The attitude of the Continental Army, as expressed by its officer core, was also dictated by the contradiction between honor-bound duty and necessity. The frustration of this contradiction prevailed in the view of General Anthony Wayne. On the one hand the native Pennsylvanian sympathized with his neighbors whose property had been "stripped and insulted" by the "unattached soldiers roaming the countryside." On the other, Wayne insisted that it was the "indispensable duty" of the inhabitants to "contribute to the support of an army which was posted [to protect] their country against the depredations of the enemy." [83] In fact Washington's staff was composed of officers who represented both sides of the dichotomy.

There were those in the high command who felt an affinity for the harassed citizenry of Valley Forge. Brigadier General Casimir Pulaski asserted that the inhabitants "have the right of first comers" and are "not inclined to supply [the army] as they are not always paid." Consistently, General Jedediah Huntington of Connecticut claimed that any army, "even a friendly one," is a "dreadful scourge to any people," for only "devastation and distress mark their steps." A sense of honor characterized the relationship of these officers to the Valley Forge residents. Some felt obliged to maintain a correspondence with their hosts after the breaking of camp. [84]

Conversely, there were those who greeted the refusal of many citizens to aid the soldiery with great animosity. Whether they were members of the Society of Friends or not, the non-complying inhabitants were castigated as "disaffected Quakers" who had no more "idea of liberty that a savage has of civilization." Having little respect for the religious scruples of Friends, Major John Clark, an intelligence officer, suggested that the local Quaker farmers be "engaged as spies of [the] condition that they should be excused from all military service and fines." [85]

Washington's attitude was much more balanced, being governed by both the responsibility he had to the welfare of his men and by his conviction that the rights of the citizens and the protection of those rights formed the basis of the American Revolution. [86] Accordingly, the Commander-in-Chief acted in a firm but just manner with both the soldiery and the citizenry. While promising the most severe discipline to those soldiers who conducted themselves poorly [87] the Virginian also directed the local farmers to thresh their grain so it would not entice the wandering soldiers and prohibited civilians from going into the City of Philadelphia in order to cut the potential flow of intelligence to the British. [88] Washington emerges here as a level-headed and responsible leader, most capable of maintaining a proper perspective of the military and civilian roles in the Revolutionary movement.

Despite the fact that popular allegiance to the cause of independence from Great Britain has been identified as the prevailing sentiment among the American people, [89] an examination of the civilian population surrounding the Valley Forge encampment proves that "patriotism" was, at best, a tenuous term. In fact, those who drove wagonloads of supplies to the encampment may have been motivated by a hungry family or a pocket full of British coinage rather than the Revolutionary cause. "Compliance" did not necessarily mean "patriot" just as "neutrality" was not always synonymous with "tory." There was a broad spectrum of compliance as well as non-compliance among the Valley Forge inhabitants. Still, the event which transpired on

---

the encampment grounds is no less remarkable, for soldiery and citizenry alike experienced a mutual sufferance, whether for a religious principle, a lack of food and clothing or for independence.

Endnotes

[1] See Mason Weems, Life and Memorable Actions of George Washington (1800); J. S. Futhey & Gilbert Cope, History of Chester County (West Chester, Pa., 1881); William J. Johnson, George Washington, the Christian Patriot (New York, 1919); Henry Woodman, History of Valley Forge (Oaks, Pa., 1922); and Edward Pinkowski, Washington's Officers Slept Here (Phila., 1953). These accounts have propagated the patriotic fiction regarding the suffering of the Continental Army at Valley Forge. Some of the more popular stories include the army's march into camp in which they left a "trail of bloody footprints behind." Others detail the personal circumstances of Washington at Valley Forge; particularly the piety of the commander as he was discovered on his knees, in prayer, during the winter of 1777 - 1778. These accounts have evaded the proof of primary documentation and what historical evidence has been uncovered discounts their validity.

[2] See John F. Reed, Valley Forge, Crucible of Victory (Monmouth Beach, N.J. 1969); John B. B. Trussell Jr., Birthplace of an Army: A Study of the Valley Forge Encampment (Harrisburg, Pa., 1976); Charles Royster, A Revolutionary People at War (Chapel Hill, 1979); and Robert Middlekauf, The Glorious Cause (New York, 1983). Although Royster's work deals with the interaction between the civilian and military sectors, the "civilian" is synonymous with the "politically-active revolutionary." Nor does Rosyster examine, thoroughly the attitiude of the common man in his chapter on Valley Forge.

[3] Charles H. Browning in his work, Welsh Settlement of Pennsylvania (Phila., 1912), was the first historian to examine the demography of the Welsh Tract, which encompasses the Valley Forge area. However, the works of Jack Marietta and Barry Levy have enhanced, considerably, our understanding of the religious lives of those Welsh Quaker settlers. Marietta's work, The Reformation of American Quakerism, 1748 - 1783 (Phila., 1984), focuses on the disciplinary records of southeastern Pennsylvania's Quaker meetings. These records illustrate that 18th century Quakers witnessed a decline in their piety and one which led a younger generation to affect a spiritual reformation within the Society of Friends. This reformation resulted in the Friends' withdrawal from the mainstream of society and, hence, made possible their campaign against slavery.

Barry Levy, in his several works, emphasizes the importance of domesticity in the lives of the Quakers who settled on the Welsh Tract and in Chester county. In "Tender Plants: Quaker Farmers & Their Children in the Delawre Valley, Pa., 1681 - 1735," Journal of Family History 3 (1978): 116 - 35, Levy argues that the 17th century Quaker commitment to the nuclear family was spiritual in nature and originated the idea of the domestic household. This commitment not only inspired the Quaker migration to Pennsylvania from England but also their tendency to accumulate wealth and property in order to manitain their Quaker religiousity. He compares the domesticity of Quakers in the Delaware Valley to their Anglican counterparts in "The Birth of the Modern

Family in Early America: Quaker & Anglican Families in the Delaware Valley, Pa., 1681 - 1750," in Friends and Neighbors: Group Life in America's First Plural Society, edited by Micheal Zuckerman (Philadelphia, 1982), 26 - 64. Here Levy argues that Quaker families thrived because of their religious ideology and their community institutions which emphasized modern strategies -- love and volunteerism instead of shame and coercion -- in raising families and building communities. And, in this sense, Quakers can be viewed as the originators of the modern family in Pennsylvania. In comparison, the Anglican families of the Delaware Valley struggled to create public social order. They "floundered economically, lost much of their previous religous identity and gave less to the valley's social and economic development" than did the Quakers. Levy traces the importance of familial relations to the Delaware Valley Quaker's origins in Merionethshire and Radnorshire Wales and Cheshire England were economic scarcity and religious persecution threatened the strong family bonds they tried to create. Penn's offer of a new home in his colony, free of persecution and rich in fertile land, answered the familial needs to these British Quakers who migrated to Pennsylvania in the 1680s. This is the thesis of Levy's piece, "From 'Dark Corners' to American Domesticity: The British Social Context of the Welsh & Cheshire Quakers' Familial Revolution in Pennsylvania, 1657 - 1685" in The World of William Penn, edited by Richard S. Dunn & Mary M. Dunn (Phila., 1986), 215 - 239. These arguments form the basis of Levy's book, Quakers and the American Family: British Settlement in the Delaware Valley (New York, 1988) which attributes a large part of 17th and 18th century of the Friends' history in the Delaware Valley to Quaker domesticity, including the Pennsylvania colony's pluralism, the political crisis of the 1750s and Quakerism's legacy for republicanism.

What is truly impressive about Levy's work, though, is the challenge it offers to those historians who argue that religion was secondary to the tasks of survival in the daily household and that familial relationships were based on economic considerations, being orderly, authoritarian and unaffectionate. These historians include John Demos, A Little Commonwealth: Family Life in Plymouth Colony (New York, 1970); Philip J. Greven, Four Generation: Population, Land & Family in Colonial Andover, Massachusetts (Ithaca, N.Y., 1970); Kenneth A. Lockeridge, A New England Town: The First Hundred Years (New York, 1970); and T. H. Breen, Puritans & Adventurers: Change & Persistence in Early America (New York, 1980).

Wayne Bodle in the Valley Forge Research Report (3 vols., Valley Forge, Pa., 1980) and "This Tory Labyrinth: Community, Conflict & Military Strategy during the Valley Forge Winter" in Michael Zuckerman, Friends & Neighbors: Group Life in America's First Plural Society (Philadelphia, 1982), 222 - 250, concentrates on the relationship of the civilian population to the Continental Army during the winter encampment. He argues that the protection and property rights fo the native inhabitants became secondary to the needs of the army. Bodle maintains that Washington and British commander Howe used the civilian population as an instrument in the battle of strategy for the proper provisioning of their troops.

VALLEY FORGE COMMUNITY

⁴ See Bodle, Research Report, vol. 1; Royster, Revolutionary People, 190; John Alden,A History of the American Revolution (New York, 1969); John Shy, A People Numerous and Armed (New York, 1976); and Middlekauf, The Glorious Cause, 411 - 17. Royster calls Valley Forge a "test of national survival because it had been a test of the Army's survival amid hardships caused in large part by fellow revolutionaries." Other historians have noted the significance of Valley Forge by citing drill master Fredrich von Steuben's successful attempt to create an efficient fighting force out of the rebel army.

⁵ The area examined was the two county region surrounding the encampment, Chester county and the northwest part of Old Philadelphia county, presently Montgomery county. More specifically, the townships concentrated on include Merion, Providence, Radnor, Tredyffrin and Whitemarsh. This region will be referred to in this chapter, alternatively, as the "Valley Forge area" or as the "Great Valley." Limitations on the availability of census records, church membership personal correspondence and journal restricted the research for this study to church records, wills, inventories, deeds, and, to a lesser degree, private family papers. A primary source of information came fron the Meeting minutes of the Radnor and Chester Monthly Meetings whose jurisdiction included the Valley Forge area.

⁶ "Warrant for Survey, William Penn to Thomas Holme, Surveyor General to the Welsh Land Company of Edward Jones," March 24, 1684 in Thomas A. Glenn, Merion in the Welsh Tract (Norristown, Pa., 1986), 11. See also Walter Klinefelter, "Surveyor General Thomas Holme's map to the Improved part of the Province of Pennsylvania," Winterthur Portfolio (1970) 6:52 - 53.

⁷ "Deed, William Penn to Letitia Penn," October 24, 1701, Philadelphia County Deed Book A, 11, 405. This tract was known as the "Manor of Mount Joy." Letitia Penn and her husband, William Aubrey, never settled on the land. Instead they sold portions of the manor, the last sale being on July 10, 1730.

⁸ Grantees of the Richard Davies Company," (1682) in Glenn, Merion, 36. Many of these Welsh Friends formed the Radnor Monthly Meeting. It is also important to note that Quakers from the eastern county of Cheshire, England settled on a piece of land adjacent to the Welsh Tract. These English Quakers had a great deal of interaction with the Welsh Friends during the eighteenth century and heavily influenced the patterns discussed in Barry Levy's works on Delaware Valley Friends.

⁹ Levy, "From Dark Corners," 220 - 221. Levy shows that the median income for those Welsh Quakers of the " middling" sort who eventually settled in the Valley Forge area, was considerably lower than their English counterparts. For example, while the personal annual income for a yeoman farmer in the Merionethshire was 36.5 pounds sterling and in Radnorshire, 27 pounds sterling, the yeoman from Cambridgeshire, England was earning 180 pounds sterling a year. This discrepancy in incomes was due, in part, to the fact that the geography of southern Wales was not very conducive to farming. Frank Emery, in "The Farming Regions of Wales" in Joan Thirsk, ed., An Agrarian History of Great Britain (4 vols., London, 1981), 4:113-60, claims

89

that more than 58% of the land in Merionethshire and Radnorshire was well over 500 feet above sea level and was composed of mountainous regions where the growing season was short and cool. Under these circumstances, most of the Welsh farmers from these counties raised sheep and black cattle, living on dispersed farms that were located on very small patches of fertile territory. Additionally, high land rents and a succession of bad harvests and floods during the 1670s combined to make subsistence in southern Wales, impossible. Religious factors were just as important in leading to the Welsh migration as Friends were persecuted under Stuart rule for "assemblying together under pretense not according to the practice of the Church of England."

[10] William Penn, "Articles of Conditions & Concessions to the Inhabitants of the Welsh Tract," in Browning, Welsh Settlement, 26.

[11] Levy, Quakers & the American Family, 58 - 59, 130. Levy maintains that the Quakers viewed the concept of "conversation" as being reflective of a person's inner being and that it "communicate meaning." For Quakers, then, "conversation" included speech, behavior and non-verbal communication. They also divided "conversation" into two languages -- "holy conversation" which led to salvation and "carnal talk," the language of pride and the world, which led to corruption and death. In order to avoid the latter the Welsh Friends sought to secure environments of "holy conversation" for their children.

[12] J. William Frost, The Quaker Family in Colonial America (New York, 1973), 64 - 88.

[13] William Penn, "Some Account of the Province of Pennsylvania," in The Works of William Penn, edited by J. Sowle, (2 vols., London, 1726), II, 699.

[14] Levy, Quakers & the American Family, 130. Levy claims that the Welsh Friends also sought to achieve holy conversation by limiting the type of labor they brought into their household -- they avoided holding slaves and by devising intricate and demanding strategies to give money and land to their children.

[15] Levy, "Tender Plants," 121. Levy claims that the Welsh farms were, on an average, 40 - 45 acres. There was little land to distribute among the children and, hence, farmers could rarely keep their children from leaving for the city. However, matters changed when they came to Pennsylvania. Levy's examination of the removal certificates of the Radnor and Chester monthly meetings reveal that Quaker youths on the Welsh Tract did live and work at home or close to their parents farms when they married.

[16] Ibid., 123.

[17] See Friends Historical Association, Inventory of Church Archives, Society of Friends in Pennsylvania (Philadelphia, 1941). Every Quaker belonged to a congregation called a "Preparative Meeting" or a "Meeting for Worship." Two or three of these meetings composed a "monthly Meeting." Approximately four to eight monthly meetings formed a "Quarterly Meeting," which met four times a year to discuss business matters and the three quarterly meetings in Pennsylvania -- Bucks, Chester and Philadelphia -- made up of

most of the membership of Philadelphia Yearly Meeting, the main administrative body of the Society of Friends. In Chester county alone there were 31 preparative meetings by 1756. The membership of these preparative meetings, as well as those of the monthly and quarterly meetings, is unknown. There exists only two Quaker meeting census records for Pennsylvania for the preiod 1682 - 1783, however, one of these is a 1688 census for Chester Monthly Meeting and discloses a membership of between 538 - 561. Most of the Friends in the immediate region of the Valley Forge encampment belonged to Radnor Monthly Meeting, whose membership was probably comparable to that of the Chester Monthly Meeting, and attended the Valley Friends Preparative Meeting.

[18] "Discipline of Philadelphia Yearly," (1722), Philadelphia Yearly Meeting Minutes, Friends Histoical Library, Swarthmore, Pennsylvania (hereafter known as "FHL"). An examination of the Radnor and Chester Meetings, 1722-40, reveals an almost infallible adherence to the directive of Philadelphia Yearly Meeting for marrying within the Society of Friends.

[19] Radnor Monthly Meeting Minutes: 12 mo./12/1711, FHL.

[20] "Arrivals, 1680-1750," in Haverford Monthly Meeting Minutes: 5 mo./4/1730, FHL.

[21] Chester Monthly Meeting Minutes: 7 mo./7/1692, FHL; and George Thomas, Diary, 11 mo./22/1794, privately owned by R. Hoopes, Gladwyne, Pa. These schools were conducted on the grounds of Darby, Haverford and Radnor Monthly Meetings.

[22] J. Oldmixon, The British Empire in America (London, 1708), 1, 303; See also William Penn, "A Further Account of the Province of Pennsylvania and its Improvements," (1685), The Pennsylvania Magazine, IX, (1885): 54-55.

[23] See Stevenson W. Fletcher, Pennsylvania Agriculture & Country Life, 1640-1840 (Harrisburg, Pa., 1971), 323; See also Glenn, Merion, 187-204. An examination of the wills and inventories of the residents of Chester and Old Philadelphia counties, for the period 1713-1730, reveals that two to four servants appear to be the average. One inventory lists as many as seven. Welsh Friends employed indentured servants because of their moral distaste for Black slavery and their quest to maintain "holy conversation" in their community. In fact, these Welsh Friends were among the first Quakers to voice their opposition to slavery, bringing it to the attention of the Chester Quarterly Meeting in the Early 1710s.

[24] Frederick B. Tolles, Meeting House and Counting House, The Quaker Merchants of Colonial Philadelphia, 1682-1763 (Chapel Hill, 1948), 51-62. Tolles traces the Quaker work ethic to the Puritan-Calvinist doctrine and the rise of modern capitalism. Quakerism, being an outgrowth of the Puritan Revolution of the mid-seventeenth century, shared a common strain of religious and economic ideas with Puritanism. One of these provided that the earning of money, with certain precautions, is allowable.

[25] Levy, Quakers & the American Family, 237. For inventories of some of the inhabitants who resided on the Valley Forge encampment grounds see

91

"Records of Administration" Evan Bevan, March 30, 1747, #4 Book F, 51; David Evans, October 20, 1763, #41 Book G, 370; Stephen Evans, County, Philadelphia City Hall Annex; and "records of Administration," Issac Walker, March 5, 1755, Register of Wills, Chester County, Chester County Courthouse. To gain a rough estimate of the wealth of these inhabitants see Jackson T. Main, The Social Structure of Revolutionary America (Princeton, 1965), 72-80. Main claims that, during the Revolutionary era, 1765-83, "laborers" were at the bottom of the economic scale, owning property worth less than 50 pounds. Rarely did a laborer own land as evidenced by the fact that one in every five laborers in Chester county had real estate. The median personal estate, in that county, was 150 pounds currency and, though it is difficult to assess the estate of a farmer, they being found on every economic level, a Pennsylvania farmer was worth approximately 400 pounds currency. Consequently, any individual with an estate worth 600 pounds currency or above could be considered a person of substance. The average value of each of the above mentioned estates was 800 pounds currency.

[26] "Deed, William Penn by his Attorneys James Logan & William Logan to Stephen Evans and Daniel Walker," February 3, 1742, Philadelphia County Deed Book G3, 97-101; "Advertisement," Pennsylvania Gazette: April 4, 1751; Arthur C. Binning, Pennsylvania Iron Manufacturing in the Eighteenth Century (Harrisburg, Pa., 1973), 32-41; Goerge Schultz, "Forges along the Valley Creek," Picket Post, (July 1946): 49-54.

[27] "Inventory of John Potts," (1786) in Potts' Family Papers, II, Historical Society of Pennsylvania (hereafter known as "HSP").

[28] Levy, Quakers & the American Family, 218. During the mid-eighteenth century the Pennsylvania Assembly created a tax category known as "freemen" in order to discourage stubborn bachelors. They were taxed at a very high rate as long as they remained unattached. All those bachelors over twenty-one years of age, working for themselves -- and not for their parents -- were eligible for this category.

[29] Ibid., 237-38.

[30] See the Reverend Evan Evans, "The State of the Church in Pennsylvania" (1707) in Harold D. Eberlein & Cortlandt Van Dyke Hubbard, The Church of St. Peter's in the Great Valley, 1700-1940 (Richmond, Va., 1944), 5.

[31] This defection of Welsh Friends occured at a time when the larger Society of Friends was experiencing a schism led by a former member, George Keith. These "Keithian Friends," as they were called, were receptive to the Anglican preaching and many urban Philadelphia Quakers, as well as the rural Friends of the Philadelphia area, defected to the Church of England. It should also be noted that during the colonial period, American Quakers, regardless of an urban or rural background, were commonly affected by the religious events of the time and held essentially the same beliefs.

[32] See Reverend Henry M. Muhlenberg, The Journals of Henry M. Muhlenberg (4 vols., Phila., 1942), 1, 72. In his entry of "June, 1750"

Muhlenberg indicates that many German Lutherans were indentured servants to the English and Welsh Quakers of Chester county.

[33] See Proceedings of the Philadelphia Presbytery: April 22, 1740, May 27, 1741, March 31, 1761, April 16 1761 and January 3, 1769, Presbyterian Historical Society, Philadelphia, Pa.

[34] See Reverend Willam Currie to the Society for the Propagation of Gospel, July 7, 1740 in Eberlein & Hubbard, St. Peter's, 49-50; For further information on the First Great Awakening see William G. MsLoughlin, Revivals, Awakenings and Reform (Chicago, 1978). McLoughlin attributes the Awakening to changing structures of authority and power in society; a shift from a "medieval, corporate, organicideal of social order" to a "modern, individualistic, contractual, atomistic social order."

[35] Muhlenberg, Journals, I, 72.

[36] See Radnor Monthly Meeting Minutes & Chester Monthly Meeting Minutes for the period 1740-1770, FHL.

[37] Chester Quarterly Meeting Minutes: 2 mo./ 9/ 1778; Radnor Monthly Meeting Minutes: 2 mo./ 8/ 1771, 4mo./ 6/ 1775, 1mo./ 12/ 1779 and 3 mo./11 /1779, FHL.

[38] Radnor Monthly Meeting Minutes: 12 mo./ 14/ 1769; Chester Monthly Meeting Minutes: 10 mo./ 20/ 1776 and 12 mo./ 30/ 1776. These incidents of fornication may have been due, in part, to the custom of "bundling." This custom, carried over from the Old World, permitted a suitor and his sweetheart to conduct their wooing in bed, during the winter months, provided that they did not remove their clothing or engage in sexual intercourse. This was a common practice among the rural groups in the Middle Atlantic colonies and, in Pennsylvania, the custom prevailed into the nineteenth cehtury.

[39] Marietta, Reformation, 56.

[40] William Logan to Sussanna Fothergill (1755) in Memoirs of the Life & Gospel of Samuel Fothergill edited by George Crosfield (Liverpool, 1858), 189.

[41] Marietta, Reformation, 40-42.

[42] Samuel Fothergill (1755), Memoirs, 281-282.

[43] Marietta, Reformation, 51-80. According to Marietta, Samuel Fothergill, John Woolman and John Churchman, who was the most spiritually active Quaker minister in Chester county, began the reformation in September 1755 at Philadelphia Yearly Meeting. These three Friends were the motivating force on a committee of fourteen which revised the disciplinary code admonishing elders, overseers and all others active in the discipline to be "zealously concerned for the cause of the Truth and honestly to labor to repair the breaches too obvious in many places that there may be some well grounded hopes of the primitive beauty and purity of the Church may be restored." To comply with this advice, the Yearly Meeting appointed a committee of thirty-one members to inspect quarterly and monthly meetings to see that those bodies carried out the advices of the yearly meeting. Additionally, the Yearly Meeting directed that a list of queries be read once every three months at every single meeting in its

jurisdiction and to have answers prepared for the quarterly meetings. Finally, the Yearly Meeting required that select meetings of ministers and elders be established in every monthly meeting and that they answer for their own behavior at a quarterly meeting for ministers and elders. The spiritual reformers also personally employed a number of tactics to insure reformation. For example, they often had extended travelling visitations of meetings and families, they lobbied the higher strata of Philadelphia Yearly Meeting in order to gain their unconditional support and they used a gradual, orthodox approach to reform: it began with the enforcement of conventional articles of church discipline like those prohibiting irregular marriages, fornication and drunkenness and gradually addressed the more sensitive issues such as public office-holding and, eventually, slaveholding for the few Friends that did engage in the practice. Marietta provides some evidence that the attempts of these spiritual reformers was successful in decreasing the incidence of delinquency among Friends in the Chester Quarter. From 1720 to 1745, delinquency among the Great Valley Friends rose from 30.9% to 49.6%. However, with the efforts of the reformers, the delinquency rate among Great Valley Friends dropped to 37.7% after 1755.

44 See Arthur J. MeKeel. "The Founding Years, 1681-1789," in John M. Moore, ed., Friends in the Delaware Valley (Haverford, Pa., 1981), 14-56. MeKeel points out that the Welsh Friends had been an important element in early Pennsylvania politics, taking issue against the imperial and proprietary interests. The anti-Crown sentiment of the Revolutionary period, then, may have found its roots in the early politics of the "Country Party" under David Lloyd. Moreover, the Society of Friends withdrew from politics, en masse in 1756, being concerned that it conflicted with their pacifist convictions with their responsibilities as political officials during the French-Indian War. Still there were those Friends who did participate in the political affairs of the time. Members of the Bevan, DeWees, Havard, Potts and Vaux families -- all of whom were from the Great Valley -- held political office or a military commission in the state of Pennsylvania despite their Quaker heritage.

45 Tolles, Meeting House, 4. Tolles uses this very appropriate analogy of the inward and outward plantations in order to describe the conflict among Quakers regarding a religiously-guarded life, on the one hand, and a more worldly life, on the other. Tolles concludes that, among Philadelphia Quakers, the latter overtook the former. This, however, was not the case in the Great Valley where there was a broader, more diverse religiosity among Friends.

46 The encampment area composed of a crude triangle bounded to the north, for three miles, by the Schuykill river, to the west, for 1.5 miles, by the smaller Valley Creek and to the southwest by another natural boundary extending 3.2 miles along a low ridge. The Valley Creek flowed between a 400 foot high Mount Joy and a 550 foot high Mount Misery.

47 "General Orders," December 17, 1777 in John C, Fitzpatrick, ed., The Writings of George Washington, 1745-1799 (39 vols., Washington D.C., 1933), X, 167-68; Anthony Wayne to George Washington, Wayne Manuscripts, IV, HSP; and "Defenses of Philadelphia in 1777," Pennsylvania

Magazine of History & Biography, XX, (1896) 4: 520-31 (hereafter known as PMHB). The latter contains the opinions of Washington's officer corps on where the army should be quartered or if they should proceed with a winter campaign; a very real possibility in the view of Congress.

[48] R. A. Bowler, *Logistics and the Failure of the British Army in America, 1775-83* (Princeton, 1975), 265-67. Bowler arrived at the figure of 120 days by current consumption levels for the British Army while that of the Continental Army was much worse.

[49] For a comprehensive treatment of the problems surrounding the military provisioning of the Continental Army see Erna Risch, *Supplying Washington's Army* (Washington D.C., 1891); For a better understanding of the relations between Congress and the Continental Army see E. Wayne Carp, *To Starve the Army at Pleasure* (Chapel Hill, 1984).

[50] Washington to the President of Congress, December 23, 1777 in Fitzpatrick, *Writings*, X, 192-98.

[51] Brigadier General James Varnum to Major General Nathanael Greene, February 12, 1778, *Washington Papers*, Library of Congress, Washington D.C.; See also Nathanael Greene to William Greene. March 7, 1778 in Richard K. Showman, ed., *The Papers of General Nathanael Greene* (5 vols., Chapel Hill, 1980), II, 300-304.

[52] See "Suffering of Friends," *Radnor Monthly Meeting Minutes*, 1777-78, FHL; and "Oath of Allegiance" *Pennsylvania Archives*, III, HSP.

[53] Marietta, *Reformation*, 213, 222-23, 258-59 & 347. Marietta contends that quantitative evidence proves that resistance to the Revolution was stronger among Chester county Friends than among their Philadelphia bretheren.

[54] "Remonstrance of a number of the Inhabitants of of Chester County to Benjamin Franklin Esq., President of the Supreme Executive Council of the Commonwealth of Pennsylvania," (September 1781) Manuscript #1727, Chester County Historical Society, West Chester, Pa.

[55] Anthony Wayne to wife, February 7, 1778, *Wayne Manuscripts*, IV, HSP; Account of Mary Thomas Jones, March 10, 1829 in Priscills Walker Streets, ed., *Lewis Walker of Chester Valley* (Phila., 1896), 76; Jacqueline Thibaut, *The Valley Forge Research Report* (3 vols., Valley Forge, Pa., 1982), III, 129-160; and J. Alden Mason, "American Officers Quarters at Valley Forge," *Tredyffrin Easttown History Quarterly*, VII, (April 1954), 28-48.

[56] Timothy Matlack to Robert Levers, May 6, 1778, *John Reed Collection*, Valley Forge National Historical Park. The properties of 15 tories were seized to house officers of the Continental Army.

[57] John W. Jordan, ed., "Moore Family of Moore Hall" in *Colonial Families of Philadelphia* (New York, 1911), 1154.

[58] "An Account of Sundry Effects taken from Friends of the Valley Preparative Meeting by the Contending Armies," in *Radnor Monthly Meeting Minutes*, 1778, FHL; "Burial List of Valley Friends Meeting, 1818," FHL; "Receipt given by Samuel Richard to Lt. Williams for 2 dollars in order to move the sick of the 13th Virginia Regiment to Valley Meetinghouse," December 20,

1777, HSP; and Mrs. Philip E. LaMonyan, The DeWees Family Papers (Valley Forge, Pa., 1902), 18.

[59] See Streets, Walker, 76; LaMonyan, DeWees Family, 18; and Chalkley T. Matlack, ed., Brief Historical Sketches Concerning Friends Meetings Past and Present (Moorestown, N.J., 1938), 520.

[60] William Davis to ? , April 1778, Washington Papers, Library of Congress; James Lovell to ?, January 5, 1778, Burnett Collection, Harvard University Library; Bodle, "Tory Labyrinth," 222-50.

[61] Captain Bejamin Bartholomew, Burial Records, 1711-1800, Church Archives, Great Valley Baptist Church, Devon, Pa.

[62] See Church Membership, 1711-1800, Church Archives, Great Valley Baptist Church, Devon, Pa.

[63] Reverend Hugh David, "History of the Great Valley Baptist Church," in Church Records, 1711-1800, Church Archives, Great Valley Baptist Church, Devon, Pa.

[64] See Burial Records, 1700-1800, Church Archives, St. Peter's Episcopal Church, Paoli, Pa.; and Burial Records, 1700-1800, Church Archives, Great Valley Presbyterian Church, Malvern, Pa.; Davis' diary is one of the most important records of the southern campaign.

[65] See Thompson Westcott, Names of Persons Who Took the Oath of Allegiance to the State of Pennsylvania, 1777-89 (Phila., 1865), 27; and "Claim of Col. William DeWees," February 11, 1794, National Archives, Washington D.C.

[66] General William Howe to Lord Germain, August 30, 1777, Sackville-Germain Papers, William L. Clements Library, Ann Arbor, MI.

[67] Captain Ca+leb Gibbs, "Washington's Valley Forge Account Book," June 18, 1778, Washington Papers, Library of Congress; Mason, "Officers Quarters," 30; "Orders of Charles Stewart, Commisary General of Issues to Captain Greenleaf," December 22, 1777, Manuscripts Collection, Massachusetts Historical Society, Boston, MA; and John Van Norden & Henry Steits of General Wayne's Division to Col. Clement Biddle, Commissoiner of Forage, December 17,1777 in Streets, Walker, 76.

[68] "General Order," January 1778 in Fitzpatrick, Writings of Washington, X, 404; Pennsylvania Packet: March 4, 1778, 1; and Massachusetts Independent Chronicle: March 5, 1778, 3. Washington claims that he will open the market in early February and that the inhabitants will "receive pay for the articles according to the prices [set by the army]." He also informs that the inhabitants "will not have liberty to receive from the soldiery any kind of clothing or military stores in pay for their provisions." This directive given both " for [the civilian's] advantage and from a regard to the accomadations of the Army."

[69] "General Order," December 25, 1777 in Fitzpatrick, Writings of Washington, X, 205; Lord Stirling to Washington, December26, 1777; John Jameson to Washington, December 31, 1777; John Clark to Washington, December 30, 1777, Washington Papers, Library of Congress; Jedediah

VALEY FORGE COMMUNITY

Huntington to W. A. Huntington, March 6, 1778, Connecticut Historical Society, New Haven, Connecticut; and "Petition of John Johnson," June 9, 1778, William Oldridge Collection, Colorado College. Despite their efforts at looting, these soldiers found it difficult to satisfy their hunger as much of the forage surrounding the encampment had been exhausted by the British before the Continentals could send out special commissary and threshing detachments. According to Harry E. Wildes in The Delaware (New York, 1940), 217, storehouses in the area "were completely empty, barns contained no cattle" and "the copious harvests of the autumn had been consumed."

[70] James Varnum to Nathanael Greene, February 12 1778, Washington Papers, Library of Congress.

[71] See Uwchlan Monthly Meeting Minutes: 1 mo./ 8 / 1778, FHL; Reverend Henry M. Muhlenberg to the Halle of Fathers, 1778 in Douglas MacFarlan M. D., "Revolutionary War Hospitals in the Pennsylvania Campaign, 1777-78," Picket Post (February 1958), 28. Although a principle hospital had been established for the army twelve miles from the encampment at Yellow Springs, the need for hospital facilities in the immediate area was great. By December 23, 1777 approximately 2,898 men reported sick or unfit for duty due to lack of clothing. By February 1, 1778 the number had risen to 3,989.

[72] See "Sufferings of Friends," Radnor Monthly Meeting Minutes, 1777-78, FHL; and Anne M. Ousterhout, "Controlling the Opposition in Pennsylvania during the American Revolution," PMHB, (January 1981), 3-34.

[73] Although the Quakers were not permitted, by their meetings, to register the damages incurred by the Army, many of the non-Quakers as well as those Friends who refused to obey meeting discipline did file a claim. It is also important to note that the Valley Forge inhabitants suffered at the hands of the British Army, before the winter encampment. These depradations occured in September 1777 when the Redcoats, after the Battle of Brandywine, moved through Chester county on their way to Philadelphia. Many of the items taken include grain, animals and farming utensils. For a complete record of damages see "A Register of Damages Sustained by the Inhabitants of Chester County by the Troops and Adherents to the King of Great Britian during the American Revolution," (1777) Manuscript #76569, Chester County Historical Society, West Chester, Pa.

[74] "Anonymous Memorandum," January 1778, Washington Papers, Library of Congress; and "Claim of Col. William DeWees," February 11, 1794, National Archives, Washington D.C. The initial destruction of the DeWees estate occured at the hands of the British who set fire to a Continental magazine on his property in September, 1777. However, DeWees was coerced into housing the supply base by the Continental Army despite his protestations. Moreover, his estate sustained further damage by the looting of vagrant Continental soldiers druing the encampment period.

[75] "General Order," March 20, 1778 in Fitzpatrick, Writings of Washington, XI, 118; See also Chester Quarterly Meeting Minutes: 2 mo./ 9/ 1778 and Radnor Monthly Meeting Minutes: December 25, 1777, FHL.

76 See Church Records, 1777-1781, Great Valley Presbyterian Church, Presbyterian Historical Society, Philadelphia, Pa.; and Vestry Minutes, 1776-1780, Church Archives, St. Peter's Episcopal Church, Paoli, Pa.

77 The Reverend William Currie to St. David's Vestry, May 16, 1776 in Eberlein, St. Peter's, 81.

78 Radnor Monthly Meeting Minutes, 1763-83 and Chester Monthly Meeting Minutes, 1763-1776, FHL.

79 Massachusetts Independent Chronicle: March 26, 1778; James Lovell to ?, January 5, 1778, Burnett Collection, Harvard University Library; and William Nelson, The American Tory (Oxford, 1961), 187-88. One of these rumors involves the plan of a loyalist Quaker near the encampment. This "Tory" allegedly conspired with the British Army to lure Washington into a trap. The Quaker invited Washington to dinner while simultaneously sending word of his arrival to the nearest detachment of redcoats. However, Washington outsmarted the Quaker, hanging him for treason.

80 Board of War to Thomas Wharton, October 18, 1777; Congress to the Supreme Executive Council, July 1777; and Minutes of the Supreme Executive Council, March 22, 1778, Colonial Records, XV, HSP; See also Council of Safety to Col. Smith, November 14, 1777, Chester County Historical Society, West Chester, Pa.

81 "Testimony of the People Called Quakers," Minutes of the Philadelphia Meeting for Sufferings: 1 mo./ 24/ 1775 and Chester Quarterly Meeting Minutes: 2 mo./ 9/ 1778 FHL; See also William Coats to Governor Thomas Wharton, February 2, 1778, Gratz Collection, HSP; and Arthur J. MeKeel, The Relation of the American Quakers to the American Revolution (Washington D.C., 1979). Mekeel points out that there was a rather broad spectrum of opinion among Friends as to what the Quaker role should be in the American Revolution. In fact, the Quaker position in the Pennsylvania Assembly at the out break of war could not be pinpointed as three distinct groups existed: neutrals, pro-rebel and loyalists.

82 Reverend David Jones, "Defensive War in a Just Cause Sinless," (a sermon) July 20, 1775, Church Archives, Great Valley Baptist Church, Devon, Pa. This sermon was preached before Quaker Col. William DeWees' regiment of Pennsylvania troops.

83 Anthony Wayne to George Washington, December 26, 1777, Washington Papers, Library of Congress.

84 Brigadier General Casimire Pulaski to George Washington, January 1778, Washington Papers, Library of Congress; Jedediah Huntington to father, January 7, 1778, John Reed Collection, Valley Forge National Historical Park; Marquis de Lafayette to Pastor of St. Peter's Church, May 25, 1778, Church Archives, St. Peter's Lutheran Church, Lafayette Hill, Pa.; and Major General Baron DeKalb to Abijah Stephens, April 12, 1780 in Streets, Walker, 190.

85 John Brooks to ? , January 5, 1778, Misc. Collection, Massachusetts Historical Society, Boston, MA: John Clark to Natanael Greene, January 10, 1778 in Showman, Greene Papers, II, 249-51; James Varnum to Col. Miller,

VALLEY FORGE COMMUNITY

March 7, 1778, Harvard University Library; and Benjamin Rush to Thomas
Wharton, March 9, 1778, Repository, HSP. The inconsistency of the Valley
Friends actions could have only led to the Army's suspicions. It would be
difficult for the high command to accept the Society's stated neutrality when
some of its "self-proclaimed members" were actively supporting the
Revolutionary movement.

86 George Washington to President of Congress, March 12, 1778 in
Fitzpatrick, Writings of Washington, XI, 72-74. Bodle argues, in his work,
"This Tory Labyrinth," that both Washington and Howe as commanders of
their respective armies were more concerned with the welfare of their troops
than with the "hearts and minds of the people" which took a "distinctively
secondary place." Instead their respective strategies to gain provisioning
dictated their treatment of the civilian population. Hence, the primary
association the Continential Army had with the Quaker inhabitants of Valley
Forge was as a "regional police force" which tried to segregate them from
British influence, cutting their trade with the City of Philadelphia and, in turn,
getting them to supply the Continental forces. Conversely, Howe manipulated
the rural Friends by paying them for goods in specie as opposed to the
Continental Army's rapidly depreciating paper money. By combining methods
of coercion and financial enticement, Howe attracted local produce to the
Philadelphia markets and this put the Continental Army at a great disadvantage.
Bodle concludes that the strategy worked effectively for Howe as it drained the
countryside of provisions for Washington's men and the British did not even
need to depend on foraging parties for their provisions which would have
increased the chances of a rebel attack against them.

87 "General Order," December 25, 1777 in Fitzpatrick, Writings of
Washington, X, 205; and Col. Richard Hampton, "orders," Captain Andrew
Fitch Papers, Connecticut State Library, New Haven, Connecticut.

88 "General Order," January 1, 1778, X, 242; George Washington to John
Potts, December 20, 1777, X , 176; Washington to General John Armstrong,
December 28, 1777, X; Washington to General John Lacey Jr., April 11, 1778,
XI; and Washington to Philadelphia Yearly Meeting, c. 1789-1790 in
Fitzpatrick, Writings of Washington, XXX, 415n. Ironically, who
Washington considered the Quakers "disaffected" and their intentions "evil"
before his arrival at Valley Forge, had a change of heart during the encampment
period. The hospitality demonstrated by some Friends impressed the
Commander to such an extent that he appealed to the Supreme Executive
Council for the return of the Virginia exiles; a group of twelve leading
Philadelphia Quakers who had been suspected of treason and had been sent into
exile at Winchester Virginia. Years later Washington would write to
Philadelphia Yearly Meeting, the main body of the Society of Friends: "Your
principles and conduct are well known to me and it is doing the people called
Quakers no more than justice to say that (except their declining to share with
others the burden of the common defense) there is no denomination among us
who are more exemplary and useful citizens.

89 Royster, A Revolutionary People, viii.

Chapter 4

The Lamb's War Ethic of the Free Quakers

The advent of the American Revolution presented a major dilemma for the Religious Society of Friends: *Was it possible to balance an allegiance to the government with the religious principles of the Society and do so without deviating from the Quaker Peace Testimony?* Despite their withdrawal from the colonial assembly in 1756, Pennsylvania's Quakers still exercised a considerable influence over the political life of the colony and thus had a difficult time divorcing themselves from a strong commitment to their Holy Experiment, even in a time of war. [1] Friends elsewhere were similarly affected. In New England, Quakers were compelled to choose between membership in the Society and the payment of taxes to support the revolutionary governments. As professors of peace in a time of war, American Friends found themselves floundering between competing loyalties. Complicating matters even further was the fact that the Society's discipline on the issue of non-compliance in military affairs was not always strictly observed in the past. [2]

To be certain, there was a broad spectrum of compliance and non-compliance among Quakers during the Revolutionary War. While there were some Friends who entertained pro-British sympathies and were opposed to resistence to the mother country, the majority remained neutral, in strict observance of the Peace

Testimony, regardless of their opposition to British policies. On the other hand, there were those Quakers who willingly affirmed allegiance to the Revolutionary cause when the Pennsylvania Assembly, in 1777, demanded such an action as the price of full citizenship. Others actively supported the American effort by paying taxes, helping to collect revenues to finance the war and serving on committees for defense. There were still others who joined the Continental Army as a sign of their dedication to the cause of independence. These patriotic Friends inevitably bore the consequences of their actions as 1,276 members were disowned from the Religious Society of Friends: 758 for military deviations, 239 for paying taxes and fines, 125 for subscribing loyalty tests, 69 for assisting the war effort, 32 for accepting public office and 42 for miscellaneous deviations including watching military drills and celebrating independence. [3] Among these were those who became Free Quakers, a group of Pennsylvania and New England Friends who sought to reconcile their patriotism with their religious convictions.

Little research has been done on the Free Quakers and those interpretations that do exist bring into question the sincerity of the group's commitment to Quaker values. While there are those historians who maintain that the Free Quaker "attachment to the general principles of the Society was sincere as they did not care to be unchurched and they wanted the simple unclerical worship of Friends" [4], others identify the Free Quakers as "nominal Friends" who had "little interest in the maintenance of the Society's testimonies." [5] An examination of the backgrounds and writings of the Free Quaker leadership, though, reveals that the group's most politically and religiously active members sought to recapture the spirit of the early Quaker movement through their involvement in the war effort, as well as their subsequent conduct in establishing a religious body independent of the Society of Friends. For them, participation in the American Revolution was consistent with the values of early Quakerism.

Quakerism was born out of the Puritan struggle for world transformation that occured in seventeenth century England. Originally, many of the early Friends were Puritans, concerned with vital faith, total dedication in worship and a Christian remaking of the social order. Most of their insights and ethics were "often Puritan attitudes pushed to severe conclusions."[6] One such conclusion was Calvin's vision of remaking each nation for the glory of God and so the early Quakers viewed the English Civil war and the events leading to it as sacred history. This apocalyptic outlook continued to direct the beliefs and actions of Friends after 1652 when they divorced themselves from the Puritan ranks to form their own religious body.

For nearly a half century after the death of Elizabeth I, all hope of carrying out this divine commission to re-order England had been repeatedly thwarted since the Puritans had been excluded from power. Instead they were forced to endure the arbitrary rule and religious discrimination of the Stuart monarchs. Until 1640 they accepted endless compromises with the royal bishops over liturgy but when Charles I's arbitrary rule and taxation united the English merchants, Parliament and the Scots and Irish against him, the Puritan-dominated House of Commons proceeded to end Stuart absolutism. It placed severe limitations on the King's power and ended his oppressive religious regime. Subsequently, after 1640, there was increasing freedom for many different sects and free congregations in England such as the Independents, Baptists and the more scattered seeker groups.

When political deadlock between the crown and Parliament resulted in civil war, Oliver Cromwell, a simple farmer with strong Puritan convictions, united the diverse religious elements in a New Model Army. Chanting psalms as they went into battle, this band of honest, sober and well-disciplined Christian soldiers crushed the King's forces by 1645 and established an English Commonwealth based on a constitutional monarchy and religious toleration. Despite Cromwell's attempt to reconcile the various minorities -- Separatist, Independents, Presbyterian and Anglican -- and his bid to establish a constitutional monarchy around a king who refused to concede any of his power, his plans failed.   In 1647 Cromwell's officers purged Parliament of its conservative faction and, later, created a "Parliament of Saints." Ultimately, because of their attempt to establish the Kingdom of God on Earth, the Puritans wanted Cromwell to abolish the parish churches.   When he refused, Parliament disbanded itself. Thereupon, Cromwell established a Protectorate, ruling through the support of his army and a Council of State composed of more conservative elements.

While radical Puritans felt betrayed and prepared an abortive revolt against the government in 1654, other groups came to believe that the conquest of evil and the reshaping of the English nation into Christ's kingdom would not be achieved through civil war or political practice.   Some of these were seekers who began to place a greater emphasis upon inner transformation, the belief that personal involvement in seeking Christ was the only sure method of transforming the world.   The early Quaker movement emerged from this attempt to unite personal experience with world transformation. [7]

Still the early Quakers did not have a monopoly on religious truth; they were, in a very real sense "seekers" in the struggle to reshape England.   Initially, before they joined with George Fox and had to accomodate his pacifism, civil war provided the means to their search.   Each victory of Cromwell and Parliament marked another step in their search for world transformation and they sought every opportunity to hasten that process.   The ferverent desire which they displayed in war earned the first Friends the admiration of Oliver Cromwell who claimed that "to be a Seeker is to be the best sect next to a Finder, and such shall every faithful, humble Seeker be at the end." [8]   Among the early Quakers who served in the Cromwellian Army were James Naylor and William Dewsbury.   Naylor, a quartermaster in the regiment of John Lambert -- the leading radical Puritan among

Cromwell's generals -- became one of the most respected preachers in the New Model Army. [9] Others such as Isaac Penington and Edward Burrough, defended the Puritan cause in their proclamation tracts, believing that they had been "called to [support] war in righteousness for His name's sake." [10] Accordingly, Burrough exhorted others to "Put on your Armour, and gird on your sword and prepare yourselves to battel for the Nations doth defie our God. Arise, arise and sound forth the everlasting word of war and judgement in the ears of all Nations. Wound the Lofty, and tread under foot the Honourable of the earth." [11] Even George Fox, the founder of Quakerism who later espoused pacifism, openly promoted the puritan idea of a Holy War against popery: "Invite all them that professe against the Pope in all Nations, to join with thee against him, and do not loose thy Dominion nor authority . . . and let thy soldiers go forth with a free willing heart, that thou may rock Nations as a cradle." [12] To be certain, the early Friends were heavily influenced by the chaotic impulses of antinomianism, apocalypticism and militancy that were rampant in England during the Puritan Revolution; a period which preceded the emergence of Quakerism as an enduring and successful religious movement. However, the early Friends did not overtly reject military solutions to their millennial vision until the 1660s, eight years after the founding of the Society of Friends.

In fact, early Friends did not place an exclusive emphasis on the inward search for world transformation until 1658 with the death of Oliver Cromwell when Quaker theologians like Burrough become disillusioned with civil war as a solution to the problem of world transformation. Accordingly, he interpreted the Protector's death as a symbol "that all men might see the first cause is lost, and that zeale which his Kindred and Army had once in their hearts against Popery is extinguished and people turned to gaze after Images . . . A pity struck through me for once noble Oliver that is now dead, and then I said . . . is it ended all in this, all his former good Service for God and the Nations, all his victories . . . and his beating down Superstition." [13]

Quakers turned inward in a search for divine guidance, engaging in a personal struggle to defeat the evil they saw in the political and religious climate of seventeenth century England.   This struggle was termed the "Lamb's War," in a 1658 proclamation tract written by James Nayler, and summarizes the early Friends' understanding of the conflict between good and evil.

Nayler, like other Early Quakers, saw the world as a mass of unredeemed humanity that could only be saved if men allowed the Spirit to conquer pride and self-will; the qualities that led the Stuarts to deprive Englishmen of their political and religious rights.   After the failure of the Puritan Revolution, Friends understood that if they were going to prepare for the Kingdom of God on Earth they would have to begin with the transformation of the individual, only then would they be able to transform society.   And so Nayler encouraged men to conquer evil by surrendering their own wills to the constant judgement and guidance of Jesus Christ, the Lamb:

> God doth nothing . . . but by his Son, the Lamb
> . . . His appearance in the Lamb . . . is to make
> war with the God of this world, and to plead
> with his subjects concerning their revolt from
> him their Creator. . . The manner of this war is,
> first . . . he gives his Light into their Hearts,
> even Men and Women, whereby he lets all see . .
> . what he owns and what he disowns . . . that so
> he may save all that are not willfully disobedient.
> They are at war against whatever is not of God
> whatever the flesh takes delight in, and whatever
> stands in respect of persons. With the spirit of
> judgement and with the spirit of burning will he
> plead with his enemies; and having kindled the
> fire and awakened the Creature and broken their
> peace and rest in sin, he waits in patience to
> recover the Creature and slay the Enmity by
> suffering all the rage and envy . . . that the
> creature can cast upon him and he receives it all
> with meekness . . . returning Love for hatred.
>
> . . . The Lamb wars in whomsoever he appears
> and calls them to join with him herein with all

> their might . . . that he may form a new man, a
> new heart, new thoughts, and a new obedience
> and there is his Kingdom . . . Do you deny
> yourselves of your pleasures, profits, ease and
> liberty that you may hold forth a chaste . . . life
> of gentleness, faithfulness and truth? Is this your
> war and these your weapons? [14]

Nayler's tract demonstrates that the ethical standards of the early Friends were based less on love and serenity than on the personal experience of an inward, albeit painful, struggle. The apocalyptic language from Daniel and the Book of Revelations reminded Friends that pain came with the realization of one's sins and self-will in the inward struggle and that the source of this pain was the Inner Light of Jesus Christ itself.

Obedience to this indwelling light of Christ was central to the process of individual and world transforman for the first Friends. Isaac Penington was so moved by this spirit that he vowed, in 1660, to follow it wherever it would lead whether that be to wage war or peace:

> I begin to yield up myself somewhat freely into
> the hands of this unknown potter to mold me into
> what he himself has a mind. I am weary of and
> much weaned from my own will and desires . .
> . and now begin to listen to this hidden power
> which I know not, yet feel working in me.

> . . . Let not me nor any else be what we would,
> but what thy will pleaseth to have us; and fulfill
> thy whole will and counsel upon us without
> giving us the least account of it until thou
> pleasest. If thou wilt lead us into folly, death,
> battle, anything, everything do what thou wilt,
> carry us whither thou wilt. [15]

For the early Quakers, then, obedience to the Inner Light was the only fixed position in their theology, everything else became secondary. The physical action was much less important than the divine guidance directing it. Consequently, while the

Quaker mission to re-make the world in Christ's eyes continued to be phrased in the apocalyptic language and symbolism of the Saints in Cromwell's Army as they rid England of the Royalists, it became increasingly inspired by the guidance of the Inward Light of Christ, the Lamb.

For the Free Quakers, the War for American Independence was no less a quest for world transformation than the English Civil War was for their Quaker forefathers. Their cause, like that of the early Friends, was triggered by the British government. In its attempt to re-organize its North American empire, Great Britain levied a number of navigation acts and sent a corps of royal officers to implement them. Americans interpreted these actions as an attempt, by the British government, to consolidate economic and political control over the colonies. They sought to dissolve the imperial connection and to establish a new, democratic system based on popular government and the exercise of free trade. This Democratic experiment had no precedent in world history and yet some Quakers, like many Americans, believed that to defend the "principles of this [type of] government" was "justified under God." [16] Those Friends who would become instrumental in the founding of the Free Quaker Society, in the 1780s, were among the strongest advocates of such an American Democracy.

Samuel Wetherill Jr., the founder of Free Quakerism, supported the American desire to determine its own political and economic destiny. A recorded minister and one who was "well respected among the membership" of Philadelphia's Fourth Street Meeting, Wetherill was also one of the City's weavers and served as manager of the United Company of Pennsylvania Manufacturers. When the Stamp Act was passed by the British Parliament, in 1765, this Quaker minister supported the non-importation resolutions in order to crush it. During the war his textile factory furnished the Continental Army with cloth for uniforms and later, in 1779, Wetherill affirmed allegiance to the state of Pennsylvania, thereby renouncing any loyalty to Great Britain. [17]

Owen Biddle was another Philadelphia Quaker who became involved in the Revolutionary conflict. A Philadelphia merchant who signed the non-importation resolutions of 1765, Biddle became quite active on the state's Committee of Public Safety and, later, on the Board of War. In June of 1777, he was appointed Deputy Commissioner of Forage for the Continental Army and quickly earned the respect of Generals Washington and Greene. Together with Samuel Foulke, a member of the Richland Monthly Meeting of Bucks County, Biddle was one of the most financially astute backers of the Free Quaker movement. [18]

Christopher Marshall and Timothy Matlack were the most radical of the Free Quakers. Disowned by Philadelphia Monthly Meeting some time before the outbreak of hostilities with Great Britain, both men joined the radical wing of Philadelphia's Revolutionary movement. [19] They became strongly opposed to the conservative leadership of John Dickinson and the Pennsylvania Assembly and "resolved to replace [them], including the constitution of the province -- the whole regime -- with a new, more liberal system." Moreover, both men commanded the political influence to achieve their goals. Both served on the Council of Public Safety and Matlack held posts, at various times, as the clerk of the Continental Congress and as the Secretary of the Supreme Executive Council of Pennsylvania, a body which assumed the executive functions of the state after the adoption of Pennsylvania's new constitution in 1776. [20]

Timothy Davis completes the circle of Free Quaker leadership. A member of Sandwich Monthly Meeting in Massachusetts, Davis challenged the Society of Friends' refusal to pay war taxes in his pamphlet entitled *A Letter from One Friend to Some of His Intimate Friends on the Subject of Paying Taxes (1775).* He became the acknowledged leader of the Free Quaker movement in New England through his visititation and correspondance with Samuel Wetherill Jr. [21] Unfortunately, for them, the Society of Friends denounced these Quakers for their patriotic actions.

The great emphasis the Society placed on the peace testimony, during the American Revolution, made it a cause for disownment to "participate in civil government in any way" since the authorities in power were "founded and supported in the Spirit of wars and fighting." [22] Accordingly, the actions of these Free Quakers earned them the disapproval of their respective yearly meetings. If they had not already been disowned, as in the cases of Marshall and Matlack, the Society of Friends removed them from its membership for "deviating from the ancient testimony and peaceable principles of Friends." [23] The irony here rests with the fact that the Free Quakers genuinely believed that they were following the "ancient principles" of the early Friends.

Like the early Friends, the Free Quakers emphasized the primacy of the Inner Light as a guide for all of their actions. They admittedly had "no new doctrines to teach, nor any design of promoting schisms" between Friends, rather they sought to "pay a due regard to the principles of our [Quaker] forefathers and to their rules and regulations so far as they apply to our circumstances."[24] (See Appendix #1) And the circumstances of their time, together with their obedience to the Inner Light, led them to participate in the American Revolution; even at the risk of being disowned by the Society of Friends. Thus, the leaders of the Free Quaker movement constantly emphasized the righteousness of their cause by appealing to the Inner Light and encouraging their followers to do the same. Addressing those Friends who were disowned by Philadelphia Yearly Meeting for their participation in the Revolution, Timothy Davis reminded them that "the Light of Jesus, which we profess is unchangeably one in all and brings all that obey it into the way of humility, purity and truth." He further exhorted these fighting Friends to "give all diligence continually to walk in the divine Light" and to let a "holy reverence possess our spirits before him in all of our actions." [25] Wetherill, likewise, gave testimony to other Friends that obedience to the Inner Light superceded all other concerns and, at times, could lead to persecution by others:

> It is now many years since the Lord in a way not less than miraculous, visited my soul with his Love and Light, giving me to see a beauty in a virtuous life far greater than anyone can comprehend . . . This prospect ravished my soul and begot in me so ardent a love to the Lord as that I then knew and felt, what it was that supported the martyrs in the flames; for I thought, if I had then an hundred lives, I could have sacrificed them all, if it had been required, for the Testimony of Jesus. At this time I entered into covenant with my God, and made a total consecration of my heart to him. [26] (See Appendix #4)

Not only did Wetherill defend his participation in the American Revolution but also his establishment of a Free Quaker Society by maintaining that since the day he made his covenant with Christ he had tried to "act by example and by precept to recommend to mankind those things on which their felicity depends." [27]

By following the leading of the Inner Light and using the same apocalyptic language that characterized the proclamation tracts of the early Friends, the Free Quakers wrote that the Revolutionary conflict against Great Britain was "intended by Heaven to be a means of effecting a reformation of life, moral and religious among people in general." Even more important, this "general reformation [could] not take place before the members of any Church militant came to experience the Love of God to be the ruling principle in them, to be the spring and motive of their actions." [28] Through a divine obedience to the Light, then, the Free Quakers would come to realize a reformation of American society. They genuinely believed that such a reformation would take place and when it did America would be "destined to be the great empire over all this world." [29] Any who stood in the way of this process, whether they be the Society of Friends or the British government, were considered to be intent on the "destruction of the liberties and freedom of this new world" they hoped to create. [30]

Essentially, both the Free Quaker and early Quaker movements were based on the fusion of personal experience and a transformation of the society in which each group lived. Their political and religious freedoms would be respected in the new world they hoped to create since it would be directed by the Spirit of Christ. To guarantee the creation of such a society, both the Free Quakers and early Friends looked inwardly for personal revelation. For them, the actions they took in affecting this transformation were less significant than the assurance that those actions were inspired by the Inner Light of Christ. Under these circumstances, defensive warfare or compliance with the government in power were justified by the common cause of both movements.

Originally, Quaker involvement in governmental and military matters was left to the individual's conscience. The sacredness of conscience, for the early Friends, was intimately tied to their conviction in the Inner Light of Christ. According to William Dewsbury, the "righeous law of God" was, in fact, revealed to Quakers through the manifestation of "the pure light in the conscience." [31] Edward Burrough maintained that religious liberty itself was basically each man's freedom to tell and respond to God's truth and, hence, persecution is evil because "the lordship over conscience is God's alone." [32] Their respect for the sacredness of conscience, as it was highly influenced by the Inner Light, made service in the New Model Army a very attractive method of affecting world transformation for the early Quakers. Cromwell himself agreed with the first Friends on this issue. In 1645, after the victory of his New Model Army against the Royalist forces at Naseby, Cromwell urged Parliament to grant liberty of conscience to the honest men who had been fighting: "He that ventures his life for the liberty of his country, I wish he trust God for the liberty of his conscience, and you for the liberty he fights for." [33]   To be certain, many of the first Friends were soldiers in Cromwell's army and viewed their participation as an attempt to defend their religious liberties. [34]

Isaac Penington, the leading mystic of the early Quakers, admitted that while the ultimate Christian ideal is one of turning the other cheek, defensive warfare may be necessary at times when religious liberty is threatened:

> Magistracy was intended by God for the
> defence of the people and their liberties; not only
> of those who have ability, and can fight for them,
> but of such also who cannot, or are forbidden by
> the love and law of God written in their hearts so
> to do . . . I speak not against any Magistrates
> or People's defending themselves against foreign
> invasions, or making use of the sword to
> suppress the violent and evil-doers within their
> own borders (for this the present state of things
> may and doth require, and a great blessing will
> attend the sword when it is borne uprightly to
> that end, and its use will be honourable; and
> while there is need of a sword, the Lord will not
> suffer that government, or those governors, to
> want fitting instruments under them for the
> managing thereof, who wait on him in his fear to
> have the edge of it rightly directed), but yet there
> is a better state, which the Lord hath already
> brought some into, and which nations are to
> expect and to travel towards. [35]

Not only is the above quotation indicative of the early Quaker belief in defensive warfare, but it also suggests that the Inner Light or "love and law of God written in [one's] heart" can lead the individual to peace as well as to war. Neither position was considered a fixed doctrine among the first Quakers. Here Penington underscores the emphasis that the early Friends placed on the leading of the Inner Light rather than the action that followed that leading. The personal experiences of George Fox serve as further illustration of that principle.

Fox viewed military service as an occupation and one which he felt divinely led to refuse. His choice was a matter of obedience to the Inner Light and to the manifestation of that light in his own conscience. When, in 1650, Fox was given the choice to be placed in a House of Correction or to be free of imprisonment on the condition that he join Cromwell's army, the founder of Quakerism rejected military service. He recorded the experience as an example of Christ's leading in his <u>Journal</u>:

> Now the time of my commitment to the House
> of Correction being nearly out, and there being
> many new soldiers raised, the commissioners
> would have made me captain over them; and the
> soldiers cried they would have none but me. So
> the keeper of the House of Correction was
> commanded to bring me out before the
> commissioners and soldiers in the marketplace;
> and there they offered me that preferment (as they
> called it), asking me if I would not take up arms
> for the Commonwealth against Charles Stuart? I
> told them that I knew from whence all wars
> arose, even from the lust, according to James'
> doctrine; and that I lived in the virtue of that life
> and power that took away the occasion of all
> wars . . . I am not to dispute of God and
> Christ, but to obey Him. [36]

The necessity of decision here compelled Fox to turn inwardly for guidance. He was led to reject a rather attractive solution to his dilemma on spiritual grounds. This he did not do out of a blind acceptance for peace but because he could not associate himself with the spirit from which war came and because of the affirmation of his inner leading. By doing so, he established a conviction about war that he had not consciously held before this time. That conviction became formally known as the Peace Testimony.

Although the Religious Society of Friends would later elevate the Peace Testimony to a religious doctrine, it is important to note that for the early Friends pacifism was nothing more than a secondary position; the only fixed doctrine was that of the Inner Light. To be sure, the Inner Light inspired Fox's pacifism but that is not to say that it did the same for other early Quakers. More important, Fox's statement on pacifism in 1660 was an attempt to ward off Quaker persecution under the restoration, monarchy.

When Charles II was restored to the throne in 1660, he issued the Declaration of Breda, promising "liberty to tender consciences" and to honor "differences of opinion in matters of religion" on the condition that they "do not disturb the peace of the kingdom." [37] To guarantee the peace and to quell the underground opposition that existed, Charles required his subjects to take an oath of allegiance to the crown. Friends naturally refused to take any oath as a testimony to their single standard of truth-telling. Their refusal appeared to reinforce the suspicions of the crown that Quakers, like some of the other extreme religious sects in England, were a subversive group intent on overthrowing the government in order to create their own vision of the Kingdom of God on Earth. Consequently, for the next twenty-five years, Quakers were imprisoned it appears more for their refusal to take the oath than for anything else. Therefore, in order to remove this suspicion, Friends, with the encouragement of Fox, wrote the Peace Testimony. By "utterly deny[ing] all outward war and strife" and admitting that the "Spirit of Christ, by which we are guided, will never move us to fight and war against any man with outward weapons, neither for the Kingdom of Christ nor the kingdoms of this World," they arrived at a practical solution to a political problem. [38]

Despite his aversion to war, Fox still supported civil government. In a 1659 epistle the Quaker founder advised Friends that they could pay taxes in order to "pay their tribute" to government while refusing to "bear and carry carnal weapons to fight with." By doing so, Friends could "keep the peace" and still "better claim their liberty." [39] For the early Friends, then, there appeared to be no contradiction between their theology and compliance with the government in power. If there was a sensitive issue in the Quaker relationship with civil government, it rested with military participation and the decision here was a matter of the individual's conscience as it was inspired by the Inner Light.

Similarly, for the Free Quakers, involvement in civil government and military matters was viewed as an moral obligation and one that was inspired by the leading of the Inner Light. Samuel Wetherill, Jr. quite logically related his patriotism to his theology as he believed that Friends "should be as watchmen on the wall as there is something due from us to the cause of independence as well as to the Lord." [40] Christopher Marshall agreed, being firmly "convinced of [his] ethical position" as a participant in the Revolutionary movement. His confidence was bolstered by his claim that "many of the stiff Quakers who maintained the testimony on peace were ashamed of their position since the engagement in New England." (i.e., the battles of Lexington and Concord) [41]

In words that echoed the early Quaker Isaac Penington, Free Quaker Timothy Matlack advocated military participation in defensive warfare. Matlack, who served in the Continental Army at the Battle of Princeton, viewed all government as "essentially a defensive war for the protection of public peace," and when it is threatened by domestic treason or foreign invasion "it then becomes the plain duty of every man to join the public defense by all means possible." If war is the consequence, participation "in such instances is not merely justifiable but right and proper." [42] Nor were the Free Quakers at a loss when they looked to the early Friends for support on the payment of taxes in a time of war. Timothy Davis, in his pamphlet *A Letter from One Friend . . .* (1775), justified the payment of taxes to the Revolutionary government, by claiming that any persons receiving benefits

116

from a government "ought to bear his proportion of the charges of it" or else they should "have no recourse to it in any case whatever." In defending his thesis Davis referred to the writings of George Fox, Isaac Penington and other seventeeth century Quakers. [43]

Like their Quaker ancestors, the Free Quakers viewed compliance in governmental and military affairs as a matter dictated by the leading of one's moral conscience. By their involvement, the Free Quakers had "no design to form new doctrines of faith" but only to "appeal to that divine principle breathed by God into the hearts of all, to leave every man to think and judge for himself, and to answer for his faith and opinions only to the sovereign Lord of conscience." [44] The exercise of an "enlightened conscience" was also sacred to these eighteenth-century Friends and so they made it a fundamental principle of their discipline to uphold the liberty of conscience: "Neither shall a member be deprived of his right among us on account of his differing in sentiment from any or all of his bretheren, he being accountable only to the Lord."[45] (See Appendix #5) To refuse to respect this moral conscience, as the Society of Friends was doing with its testimony on peace, was to ignore the fundamental doctrine of Quakerism itself; something the Free Quakers were quick to emphasize to their former brethern.

In supporting his position Wetherill pointed to the hypocrisy of Philadelphia Yearly Meeting in disowning members who encouraged freedom of conscience and action in their attempt to respect the leading of the Inner Light:

> . . . let us now enquire into the nature
> of that offence which was esteemed of such
> magnitude as to render it necessary to testify
> against us. It was simply for submitting to the
> dispensations of Divine Providence, which you
> yourselves have since done, for this no offence,
> have we been and are still to be held up by you in
> an odious light. . . this same conduct led the
> Scribes and Pharises, who bid the Apostles be

silent, to excommunicate men for believing in
Christ. [46] [See Appendix #4]

Accordingly, the Free Quaker founder challenged the yearly
meeting to reassess the "illogic of its discipline" that "no man
should defend his own life nor the life of his friend nor the
government under which he lived, nor pay taxes for military
purpose, nor publish a religious or political treatise without the
consent of the Society, under the penalty of being expelled from
that body."[47] Timothy Davis agreed, claiming that New England
Yearly Meeting would "do themselves and their religion more
honor to erase certain tenets out of their Book of Discipline, that
higher reason, nor Scripture can support. [48] Even more sarcastic
was Marshall's claim that the Society would rather worship their
Book of Discipline than the most fundamental doctrine of the
Inner Light: "How formal in crying out the Discipline, yet how
covetous and uncharitable you are to those who follow the Light!"
he declared. [49]

What was especially alarming to the Free Quakers, though,
was the Society's indifference at "endangering religious toleration
in the state" through their "horrid intolerance against their whig
bretheren." Denied the use of meetinghouses and burial grounds
under the care of the Society, the Free Quakers sought to
publicize the illogical actions and religious discrimination of the
main body of Friends. The Free Quakers, who maintained that
they had a legal right to retain some of the properties once shared
with the Society of Friends, challenged Philadelphia Yearly
Meeting with a test case, strikingly familiar to their own situation,
to underscore the inequity of their actions:

> Suppose the state had been held by the
> Society of Quakers and that the King and
> Parliament had passed a law declaring the whole
> forfeited to him -- that the King had sent an army
> to take possession of it -- that one part of the
> Society had taken arms and repelled the invaders
> and that the others had disowned them for it.
> Would the whole right be vested in those who

> disowned the others to the total exclusion of
> those who defended it? There is no reasoning in
> such a case; every man feels at once, it could not
> be so. Nay more, every man feels that it would
> be a right that those who responded to defend,
> should be permitted to retain part of it. And if it
> cannot be so in the whole, on what reasoning can
> it be so in part? Surely, none. [50]

Essentially the Free Quakers contended that the sancitity of the Inner Light doctrine of the early Friends superceded all other testimonies of the Society. They genuinely believed that by placing a greater emphasis on the Peace Testimony, the Philadelphia and New England Yearly Meetings were denying the possibility that the Inner Light could lead the individual to participate in civil government or in a war effort. Their negligence in this matter not only served to denigrate the most fundamental doctrine of the early Friends, but it also threatened the sanctity of the individual's conscience as well as the principle of religious toleration. For these reasons, the Free Quaker leadership believed themselves to be more dedicated to the religious principles of the first Friends than the main body of eighteenth-century Quakers and, hence, declared themselves to be the *true* Society of Friends. (See Appendix #3) Indeed, the Free Quaker movement did mirror some aspects of the early Quaker theology and, like their forefaters, they were also persecuted for their beliefs.

From their beginnings, in 1652, the early Friends expected persecution for their beliefs. Even during Cromwell's Commonwealth period Quakers were imprisoned at least in 2,100 cases for contempt of court, disturbance of the peace or refusal to pay tithes. Their persecution continued during the restoration period especially under the Quaker Act which had been prompted by suspicions that they were involved in a plot, along with the Fifth Monarchist Baptists, to overthrow the government. [51] But the first Friends saw this persecution as inevitable since their Lamb's War required suffering. According to Fox: "that Spirit which makes the Just and the good and the seed of God to suffer within is the same that makes to suffer without when it is cast out within . . . and all the sufferings without is nothing to the sufferings within." [52] Rather than mourn their suffering, the early Quakers found strength in it, even celebrating the actions of their persecutors. They realized that persecution would lead to individual sanctification as the "government of the Anti-Christ is in the heart" and to destroy that government would be to rid the soul of self-will and pride, the real enemies of the Lamb's War.[53]

Early Friends also looked to each other for support in coping with persecution. A Meeting for Sufferings was established to maintain contact with those Friends who had been imprisoned for their beliefs. A network of meetings was also established throughout Great Britain in order to provide a means of fellowship with those who sympathized with the Lamb's War. George Fox's establishment of the Valiant Sixty, a group of itinerant Quaker ministers including Nayler, Burrough, Penington and Dewsbury, helped to perpetuate this Quaker network in their attempt to carry the message of the Lamb's War throughout the British Isles. Through the evangelizing of ministers like William Dewsbury, the early Friends exhorted others to prepare themselves for the coming of the Lord by purging their souls of pride and self-will and to join in this Lamb's War:

> Now is the Lord appearing in this day of his
> mighty power, to gather His elect together, out of
> all forms and observations, kindreds, tongues
> and nations; and exalting Jesus Christ to be
> Kings of Kings, to lead his Army he hath raised
> up in the North of England [i.e., the Valiant
> Sixty]; and is marched toward the South, in the
> mighty power of the living Word of God, which
> is sharp as a two-edged sword, to cut down the
> high and low, rich and poor, priests and people;
> and all the powers of the land, all the world over,
> that defiles the flesh and walks in disobedience to
> the righteous law of God, the pure light in the
> conscience...

> ...To all the saints and children of the most high
> God, whom he hath called and chosen out of the
> world, and all the customs, fashions, worships,
> forms...which are set up by the will of man to
> wait upon him in the light, the counsel of Jesus
> Christ, the Captain of our Salvation; every one in
> your measure stand valiant soldiers and be
> discouraged neither at the enemy within nor
> without, lift up your heads and behold your
> Jesus Christ, who is present with you, to dash in
> pieces and destroy all your enemies for you.
> Stand faithful in his counsel, and walk in his
> power; and be bold in the Lord for you are the
> Army of the Lord Almighty.[54]

No different was the experience of the Free Quakers who viewed themselves as being persecuted for their convictions by the Society of Friends. By disowning them and, later, denying them the use of what were once their meetinghouses, schools and burial grounds, the Society of Friends was acting no better than what the British government and Anglican Church had done to the first Friends.[55] (See Appendix #3)   And yet, Samuel Wetherill Jr., like his Quaker ancestors,   celebrated this persecution for it sanctified the Free Quakers as a religious body:

> We acknowledge the kindness of Providence in
> awakening us to a view of the deplorable
> situation in which we have been: disowned
> and rejected by those among whom we have
> been educated, and without a hope of being
> ever again united to them: separated and
> scattered abroad, as if we had been aliens in a
> strange land: the prospect of our situation has
> indeed humbled us: but that mercy which "to an
> hair's breadth," covers the judgement seat of
> God has preserved us, and induced us to
> confide that he will care for us, being made
> sensible of the indispensable necessity of
> uniting together.[56] (See Appendix #2)

Although Wetherill often became discouraged by the smallness of the Free Quaker fellowship, which never amounted to much more than 170 members, Davis reminded him that "truth is not determined by numbers" and that if the Free Quakers could "be so favored as to stand approved in the sight of God by a real sense of his divine approbation, that should be sufficient enough." [57] Additionally, Davis reminded the Philadelphia minister that the "growth and prosperity of their church depends on the sanctification and renovation of its individuals: to hold even the truth in unrighteousness hath a direct tendency to bring ourselves and the religion we profess into contempt and to cause those to perish for whom Christ died." [58] Samuel Foulke agreed with Davis, urging his Free Quaker bretheren to "examine in [their] most retired moments whether each of us wishes to do our part before a general reformation can take place" within their meeting. [59] To effect such a reformation, each member would have to surrender himself, whole-heartedly, to the leading of the Inner Light and, thus, bring himself into a more humble disposition. By doing so, the Free Quakers, as a group, would be able to purge themselves of the pride and self-will that characterized the larger Society of Friends. "There is not anything that will more effectually prepare the way for the growth of true religion," said Timothy Davis, "than a dying to pride and selfishness. When we feel the motion of the evil principle urging itself on our minds we must suppress it by turning from it to the principle of Light and Grace, which is done by humbly waiting for it with our mind inward." [60]

This denunciation of pride and self-will was reinforced by the Free Quaker belief that their separation from the Society of Friends was "not sought" by them, but rather "forced upon [them] as the pride and folly of [their] former church, vainly attempting to abridge the rights of conscience." They believed the Society to be unjustified in disowning them "for no other cause than a faithful discharge of those duties which we owe to our country." [61] Although they "lamented the loss of those advantages which arise from religious communion" with the Society of Friends, "fear[ing] a greater loss in to [their] children and families," the separation allowed them to cleanse themselves as a religious body

from the "pride and folly" that characterized the main body of
Friends. Like their early Quaker ancestors, the Free Quakers
established their own spiritual network for support. This
spiritual kinship was essential to their survival as a religious
group since it strengthened the unity of the Free Quaker
membership and permitted them to cope with the persecution
levelled against them by the Society of Friends. Timothy Matlack
reminded a fellow Free Quaker of the importance of this spiritual
kinship:

> The blessings provided for us are great and
> many and instead of being overlooked and
> disregarded, deserve the return of grateful
> acknowledgement . . . Among the things that
> are present with us some relate only to this
> world while the connection of others extend
> throughout the boundless state of endless
> existence and will pass with us into eternity.
> Our daily wants induce, generally, a sufficient
> attention to these things which nature requires
> for our bodily support and the ties of blood and
> kinship are felt and acknowledged. But these
> perish and are buried with us when we are
> brought to acknowledge our common kindred
> with the rest; while another relationship, a
> kindred of minds, often, much too often
> neglected ascends with us above the regions of
> mortality and lives where bodily connections
> are forgotten forever. This kindred it is which
> we ought to prize, to cultivate and improve
> seeing that all the others perish. [62]

Prior to their establishment as a formal body, in 1780, and
for years afterward, the Free Quakers of Philadelphia sought to
propagate their numbers and, hence, extend their spiritual
kinship, by convincing others of the righteousness of their
position. In the evangelizing spirit of the first Friends,
Christopher Marshall accused the wealthy Philadelphia Quakers
of "covetousness, grasping, worldliness, extreme pride, loftiness
and luxury." He claimed that some of these Friends were
advocates of a British government that was "inspired by the

123

Prince of Darkness," their intention being to "destroy the liberties and freedom of this new world" and to "subject it to papal power." [63] In their hope to convince others of these same ideas, as well as to promote the righteousness of their movement and to increase their membership, Timothy Matlack and Samuel Wetherill Jr. extended their missionary efforts to New England. Their epistles to these separatists were strikingly similar to those worded by the first Quakers over a century before. Referring to their persecution in the same biblical tone as the early Friends, Wetherill wrote:

> We [the Free Quakers] are weak now having been scattered abroad and lived solitary from our kindred . . . yet we feel that fraternal affection toward you which causes Esau to weep on the neck of Jacob and Jacob to weep on the neck of Esau. We feel ourselves your bretheren. We cherish a hope that there may be found among you, young men, undismayed by the chariot of fire who may have caught hold the mantle of Elijah and drawn down a double portion of the Spirit of the Great prophet upon them . . . We hope that you will adopt the name Free Quakers so we might be outwardly one people in name and practice." [64]

When Philadelphia Yearly Meeting criticized the Free Quakers for their evangelizing, Wetherill reminded them of "the liberty which their forefathers took in going into the place of worship of other societies and speaking among them." Again, Wetherill accused the Society of Friends of hypocrisy as it would have condoned the evangelism of the early Friends but refused to recognize "the duty of a person of another society to come and preach to Friends." [65] Despite the protestations of both the Philadelphia and New England Yearly Meetings, Wetherill and Matlack met with some success in their effort to promote Free Quakerism. Winning the adherence of a small separatist meeting in Massachusetts, known as the Dartmouth Monthy Meeting, the Pennsylvania Free Quakers were assured by the hope of that meeting's leader, Timothy Davis, that "a further acquaintance" between the two groups "may be of mutual advantage." [66]

During the 1780s and 1790s the Free Quakers continued their missionary efforts but failed to increase their numbers much over one-hundred-and-seventy members. Despite their failure to gain more adherents, the leadership of the group attempted to remain true to the early Quaker ethic of the Lamb's War: to battle those feelings of self-will and pride through a humble submission to the Inner Light of Christ. Accordingly, while some were led to continue their adherence to the cause of Free Quakerism, others were inspired to rejoin the Society of Friends. Timothy Matlack, for one, defended his participation in the American Revolution to his death, maintainig that the "Spirit of the Just when removed from this world to a better" will be "consecrated and relieved of their distresses." [67] Conversely, Owen Biddle resolved his conflict of conviction near the end of the war. By June, 1783 he had "made an acknowledgement" to the Philadelphia Monthly Meeting that his conduct during the Revolution was "so unguarded and contrary to the peaceable principles of Christianity" that it has "brought remorse and sorrow." He further stated that it was his "sincere and ferverent desire" to "be restored again to membership" with the Religious Society of Friends. [68]

The Society of Free Quakers would survive until 1834 when declining membership compelled the group to disband as a religious body. [69] To be certain, the Free Quakers were, in their theology, a self-destructive group. In their attempt to be "free from the restraints which characterized the main body of the Society" [70], the *Free* Quakers treated the Inner Light as an isolated doctrine, subordinating all of the Society's other testimonies. No community and no indvidual believer can do this if they seek to be part of a religious tradition. Hence, the Free Quakers failed to realize that what gives force and meaning to any doctrine is what accompanies it. Pacifism was, necessarily, a primary manifestation of the Inner Light doctrine according to the tenets of Friends. To disavow this conviction, as the Free Quakers did, was to dilute the meaning of eighteenth-century Quakerism. Simultaneously, however, the Free Quakers compelled the Society of Friends to re-evaluate its commitment to the sanctity of personal experience in following the leading of the Inner Light. By taking the fundamental doctrine of the early Friends -- the Inner Light of Christ -- and pitting it against a secondary testimony on peace, the Free Quakers illustrated a contradiction in the practice of the Philadelphia and New England Yearly Meetings in their attempt to elevate pacifism over personal experience; the basis upon which George Fox founded the Quaker religion. The Society of Friends was unable to realize that the experiences of men are not the same and that each man must confront God for himself in deciding his course of action.

When assessing the historical role of the Free Quakers, therefore, it is necessary to understand that there has always been a tension in Quakerism between the radical individualism of the Inner Light and the stabilization of that impulse in the meeting. While the collective sense generally prevails, the individual impulse usually has resources within the Quaker tradition that make it difficult to deny its legitimacy. The Free Quakers, then, were reminding the main body of Friends of their particular claim to that legitimacy by emphasizing the primacy of the Inner Light. Moreover, in their attempt to adapt the Lamb's War ethic of the early Friends to their own particular historical circumstances, the Free Quakers gave testimony to their conviction of the righteousness of the American Revolution.

Endnotes

[1] While some historians maintain that the Society of Friends replaced their political influence with benevolent reforms during the mid-eighteenth century, others argue that the Friends were politically- active through the Revolutionary period. Sydney James was the earliest spokesman for the former view. In his work, A People Among Peoples: Quaker Benevolence in Eighteenth-CenturyAmerica (Cambridge, Mass., 1963), James argues that the late eighteenth century was a time when the Society re-directed its energies away from the political sphere and into reform work in order to retain their influence in the larger society. Having failed to resolve their dilemma as ardent pacifists who also served in public office in a time of war, Quakers hoped to preserve their influence on Pennsylvania society through their involvement in anti-slavery, temperence, education and prison reform rather than governmental affairs. For James, the sphere of influence changed, but Friends still retained a strong interest in public matters. While Jack Marietta agrees with James' thesis that Friends retreated from the political sphere in order to focus on reform causes, he believes that this reform was much more tribalistic than previously assumed. Marietta's work, The Reformation of American Quakerism, 1748-1783 (Philadelphia, 1984), concentrates on the membership of Philadelphia Yearly Meeting and demonstrates that the Society of Friends "chose a sectarian course for itself" in order to "preserve their integrity" and to "purify their church." Guided by a group of religious reformers, the Yearly Meeting "showed a lack of concern for the world," believing that "a sense of divine commission" obliged them to withdraw from the public affairs of the colony. On the other hand, there are those historians who point out that the Quakers had a continuing interest in politics even after the Crisis of the 1750s. Frederick Tolles' Meeting House and Counting House: The Quaker Merchants of Philadelphia, 1682-1763 (Chapel Hill, 1948) maintains that by 1756 financial prosperity and political interest had usurped a higher place in the personal lives of Friends than did the religious testimonies of their Society. Under these circumstances only the most conscientious members of Philadelphia Yearly Meeting withdrew from Pennsylvania government, being unable to reconcile their pacifism with their responsibilities of public officials in a time of war. But even these Friends continued to pressure government, from the outside, for specific reforms. This interpretation was further clarified by Richard Bauman in the early 1970s. In his work For the Reputation of Truth (Baltimore, 1971), Bauman maintains that the trials of the Revolutionary era instigated a spiritual movement within Philadelphia Yearly Meeting that was divided along political lines. While the leaders of this reformation were those Friends who sought to maintain the highest values of the Society and who advocated a complete withdrawal from political affairs, there were those Quakers who sought to carry out their religious principles in Pennsylvania government. These "Quaker politiques" retained close ties to the Yearly Meeting and attempted to emulate the practice and beliefs of the Early Friends in their exercise of political power. A

third group, the "politicians," consisted primarily of Quaker merchants who were more concerned with financial prosperity and political prestige than with Quaker doctrine. Bauman views the late eighteenth-century as a period of internal political conflict between these three groups. Finally Richard Ryerson in his brilliant work, The Revolution Is Now Begun: The Radical Committees of Philadelphia, 1765-1776 (Philadelphia, 1978) reinforces the significant political influence of the Quakers through the Revolutionary period. In his examination of the economic status, national origin and religious faith of the men who formed the radical committees of Philadelphia, Ryerson found that while Quakers themselves did not compose the majority of Pennsylvania's Assembly, "Friends and former Friends with strong Quaker ties did hold very nearly half of the seats in the House until October 1775."

2 The Quaker dominated Pennsylvania Assembly had long assumed the ethical right to tax clonists for money for the "King's use" at times of war without compromising their pacifist principles. Everybody knew, of course, that the money was going to be used to arm, feed and pay soldiers whose duty it was to kill others. And yet this policy was followed throughout the colonial period. A comprehensive statement on the position and conduct of the Friends relative to war was not established until the autumn of 1776 when a grand council of American Quakerdom appointed a committee including Friends from all the yearly meetings in the colonies to draft such a statement. The advices of that committee was adopted by the yearly meetings and discouraged all Friends from participating in civil government in any way since the authorities in power were "founded and supported in the Spirit of Wars and fighting." Not only were Friends forbidden to bear arms but also to pay any fine, penalty or tax in lieu of personal military service, nor were they to allow their children, apprentices or servants to do so. Friends were also forbidden to engage in any business that would promote the war effort. Any infraction could result in disownment from the Religious Society of Friends. (See Philadelphia Yearly Meeting Minutes, III, 356- 57). The other American yearly meetings accepted this statement as reflecting their position.

3 Arthur J. Mekeel, The Relation of the Quakers to the American Revolution. (Washington D.C., 1979), 200-201.

4 See Charles Wetherill, History of the Religious Society of Friends Called By Some the Free Quakers in the City of Philadelphia. (Philadelphia, 1894); Rufus Jones, The Quakers in the American Colonies. (New York, 1911), 570; and Arthur J. Mekeel, "Free Quaker Movement in New England During the American Revolution," in Bulletin of Friends Historical Association. XXVII, (1938): 72-82.

5 Marietta, Reformation, 246; and Isaac Sharpless, A Quaker Experiment in Government. (Philadelphia, 1902), chapter ix.

6 Hugh Barbour, The Quakers in Puritan England. (New Haven, 1964), 2. While Barbour gains support for his thesis from Alan Simpson, Puritanism in Old & New England (Chicago, 1955) and Sydney Ahlstrom, A Religious History of the American People (New Haven, 1972), the extension of Quakerism from the Puritan Revolution is a contested issue. Melvin B. Endy

Jr. in his historiographical essay, "Puritanism, Spiritualism & Quakerism" in The World of William Penn, edited by Richard and Mary Dunn (Philadelphia, 1986), reviews the various arguments on this issue.

[7] Ibid., 1-32; See also Hugh Barbour and Arthur Roberts, (editors), Early Quaker Writings. (Grand Rapids, Michigan, 1973), 16-27; For a more comprehensive treatment of the entire period see G.M. Trevelyan, England Under the Stuarts. (1949), Lawrence Stone, The Causes of the English Revolution, 1529-1642. (1972), and Michael Walzer, The Revolution of the Saints: A Study of the Origins of Radical Politics. (1965). These seekers were not so much a distinct group as they were "spiritual orphans" or separatists who denied the existence of any true church, ministry or sacraments. Many circulated between different religions but still retained a silent, meditative worship in the hope that the Spirit of Christ would give them guidance in their quest to find the Kingdom of God on Earth.

[8] Oliver Cromwell (1648) quoted in William C. Braithwaite, The Beginnings of Quakerism. (Cambridge, 1912), 26-27.

[9] Barbour & Roberts, Early Quaker Writings, 103.

[10] Edward Burrough in his epistle to the Reader in The Great Mystery of the Great Whore Unfolded. (London, 1649).

[11] Edward Burrough, To the Camp of the Lord in England (London, 1655), 9.

[12] George Fox, MS Letter (1654) quoted in Barbour, Quakers in England, 196.

[13] Edward Burrough, The Memorable Works of a Son of Thunder and Consolation. (London, 1672), 459-61.

[14] James Nayler, "The Lamb's War" (1658) in Barbour & Roberts, Early Quaker Writings, 105 & 114-16.

[15] Isaac Penington, "Letters of Counsel" (1660) in Barbour & Roberts, Early Quaker Writings, 227.

[16] (Timothy Matlack ?) "More than One Disowned Quaker" in Pennsylvania Journal: September 14, 1782.

[17] See Mrs. S. Wetherill, Samuel Wetherill & the Early Paint Industry of Philadelphia. (Philadelphia, 1916), 1 & 6; See also Charles Wetherill, History of Free Quakers, 16.

[18] See Henry Biddle, Owen Biddle & His Descendants (n.p., 1812), HQC.

[19] The ethical behavior of Marshall and Matlack was brought into question by Philadelphia Monthly Meeting long before the Revolutionary period. Marshall, who at one time had been regarded by the meeting as a "profoundly religious individual" was disowned by the Society, in 1751, for "associating with men suspected of engaging in counterfeiting and the passing of false currency." (Philadelphia Monthly Meeting Minutes: 3 mo. / 31 / 1751) If this allegation was correct, it would be easy to understand how Marshall was able to retire from his apothecary business a wealthy man by the time of the

Revolution. Matlack's conduct was more sensational. Disowned by the Society of Friends in 1765 for "failing to pay the debts" incurred in his hardware business and for "frequenting the wrong kind of company," this Free Quaker's greatest claim to fame before the Revolution was his penchant for gambling, horse-racing and the lower class sport of cock-fighting. His hedonistic attitude, combined with his Whiggish politics, frequently earned him the wrath of the wealthier class. In fact, Matlack's tendency to offer his unsolicited political opinions resulted in a public fist fight, in 1781, when he attempted to heckle one of the most affluent Philadelphians and a fierce opponent of the radicals, Whitehead Humphreys. The vengeful Humphreys, who received the worst end of the fight, wrote and distributed a poetic broadside which reflected some of the upper class contempt for Matlack: *"Although dear Tim you've rose so great, From trimming cocks to trim the state / Yet to a brother, lend an ear, A moment -- tho' in humble sphere . . . / Did you forget in days of yore when you, like Price, was wretched poor? / But all at once you've raised so high, Quakers can't safely pass you by!"*

While Marshall and Matlack would appear to be unconcerned with the religious discipline of the Society and their compliance in the war effort might be construed as simply another offense to an already established pattern of deviant behavior, it would be misleading to dismiss these radical Friends as unconcerned in their practice of Quakerism. Their writings demonstrate that they believed their interpretation of Quakerism to be based on the spirit of the early Friends.

[20] See "Timothy Matlack" in Matlack Collection. Book 18, 43-46, Quaker Collection at Haverford College (hereafter known as "HQC"); Eric Foner, Tom Paine and Revolutionary America. (London, 1976), 109; Marietta, Reformation, 231.

[21] Mekeel, "Free Quaker Movement," 73-74.

[22] Philadelphia Yearly Meeting Minutes, III, 356-57.

[23] For Wetherill's disownment see Philadelphia Monthly Meeting Minutes: 8mo./1779; for Biddle see Philadelphia Monthly Meeting Minutes: 10 mo./27/1775; and for Davis see Sandwich Monthly Meeting (MASS.) Minutes: 12 mo./4/1778.

[24] Samuel Wetherill, An Address to Those of the People Called Quakers Who Have Been Disowned for Matters Civil and Religious. (Philadelphia, 1781).

[25] Timothy Davis, "Epistle from Dartmouth Massachusetts Free Quakers" in Free Quaker Minutes: 5 mo./15/1786, HQC.

[26] Samuel Wetherill to the Second Day's Morning Meeting of Ministers & Elders of the People Called Quakers in the City of Philadelphia, 11 mo./23/1793 in Charles Wetherill, History of Free Quakers, 98.

[27] Ibid., 99.

[28] Samuel Foulke to the Free Quakers of Philadelphia, 10 mo./1782, Friends Historical Library at Swarthmore College (hereafter known as FHL).

[29] Samuel Wetherill (1782) quoted in Charles Wetherill, History of Free Quakers, 39. In 1782 the Philadelphia Free Quakers, who had been conducting their meetings in private residences to that time, purchased a lot at Fifth and Mulbury (presentlu Arch) streets for the construction of a Free Quaker meetinghouse. When completed, in 1783, a stone was placed high in the northern gable bearing the inscription: "By General Subscription for the Free Quakers Erected in the Year of Our Lord 1783 of the Empire 8." When Wetherill was questioned about the use of the term "empire" he replied that America was destined to become the empire over all thie world.

[30] Christopher Marshall to "Friend John", January 30, 1776; Marshall to "Esteemed Friend", September 22, 1774; Marshall to "J.P.", April 13, 1775 in Marshall Letterbook at the Historical Society of Pennsylvania (hereafter known as "HSP").

[31] William Dewsbury, "True Prophecy of the Mighty Day of the Lord," (1655) in Barbour & Roberts, Early Quaker Writings, 94.

[32] Edward Burrough, The Case of Free Liberty of Conscience in the Exercise of Faith & Religion.(London, 1661), 5.

[33] Oliver Cromwell quoted in Braithwaite, Beginnings of Quakerism, 8.

[34] See Christopher Hill, God's Englishman, Oliver Cromwell & the English Revolution. (New York, 1970), 59-60.

[35] Isaac Penington, The Works of Isaac Penington. (2nd edtn., London, 1761), i, 444, 448.

[36] George Fox, The Journal of George Fox edited by Norman Penney. (2 vols., Cambridge, 1911), I, 46.

[37] William Braithwaite, The Second Period of Quakerism. (Cambridge, 1955), 8-12.

[38] Ibid., 12-18.

[39] Fox, The Works of George Fox. (New York, 1831), vii, 168-69.

[40] Samuel Wetherill quoted in Mrs. S. Wetherill, Wetherill, 8.

[41] Marshall, The Diary of Christopher Marshall, 1774-76 edited by William Duane. (Philadelphia, 1839), 26.

[42] Matlack quoted in Charles Wetherill, History of Free Quakers, 23.

[43] Timothy Davis, A Letter from One Friend to Some of His Intimate Friends on the Subject of Paying Taxes. (Watertown, Massachusetts, 1775).

[44] Samuel Wetherill, "An Address," in Charles Wetherill, History of Free Quakers, 48.

[45] Free Quakers, "The Discipline of the Society of Friends by some styled the Free Quakers," (1781) in Charles Wetherill, History of Free Quakers, 32.

[46] Samuel Wetherill, "Letter to Ministers," in Charles Wetherill, History of Free Quakers, 107.

[47] Samuel Wetherill, "An Apology," in Charles Wetherill, History of Free Quakers, 34-35.

[48] Timothy Davis quoted in Letter from Walter Spooner to Samuel Wetherill, 10 mo./ 9/1797, Wetherill Papers, FHL.

[49] Marshall to "T.H.", March 28, 1776 in Letterbook, 176-77, HSP.

[50] (Timothy Matlack ?), "More than One Disowned Quaker" in Pennsylvania Journal: September 14, 1782.

[51] See Hugh Barbour, Quakers in England, 205-7. The Fifth Monarchists were perhaps the most radical element of the Puritan Revolution. They desired the establishment of the Fifth Monarchy or the reign of Christ and His Saints which, according to the Book of Daniel, was to supercede the four monarchies of the ancient world. They were opposed, by principle, to Parliament or representative institutions of any kind and they carried out open hostilities towards the government.

[52] Fox, Journal, I , 288.

[53] Burrough, "Anti-Christ's Government," The Memorable Works, 45.

[54] Dewsbury, "True Prophecy," 93-102.

[55] After numerous appeals to Philadelphia Yearly Meeting, the Free Quakers wrote to the Pennsylvania General Assembly in order to secure their property rights to meetinghouses, burial grounds and schools. They based their appeal to the Assembly on their patriotism, declaring that "allegiance and protection are reciprocal" and that because of the support they gave to the war effort, the state should "recognize the right of the [Free Quakers] to hold in common with others of the Society of Friends the meetinghouses, burial grounds and schools held by that people as a holy body." Unfortunately for the Free Quakers, the Assembly regarded the situation as an internal matter among the Friends and neglected to act on the Free Quaker appeal.

[56] Samuel Wetherill, "Address to Our Friends & Bretheren in Pennsylvania and New Jersey," June 4, 1781 in Charles Wetherill, History of Free Quakers, 51.

[57] Davis to Wetherill, 7 mo./18/1786, Wetherill Papers, FHL.

[58] Davis to Wetherill, 10 mo./10/1789, Wetherill Papers, FHL.

[59] Samuel Foulke to the Free Quakers ca. 1781 in Scattergood, Account of Free Quakers.

[60] Davis to Wetherill, 7 mo. 23/1791, Wetherill Papers, FHL.

[61] Samuel Wetherill, "An Address," 47; See also Davis to Wetherill, 7 mo./18/1786, Wetherill Papers, FHL.

[62] Matlack to Anne Wood, October 15, 1781 in Matlack Collection, HQC. While the spiritual kinship of the Free Quakers provided the basis of their fellowship, it is important to note that they also established a secure financial network within their organization. Wetherill, Foulke and White Matlack, Timothy's brother, maintained some strong business connections among themselves. By being separated from the Society of Friends, these Free Quakers lost the benefit of doing business with their former bretheren who, according to Frederick Tolles, established a very intricate financial network within the confines of their religious Society.

63 Marshall to "Friend John," January 30, 1776; Marshall to "Esteemed Friend," September 22, 1774 in Marshall Letterbook, HSP.

64 Matlack & Wetherill, Epistle to New England Friends, 5 mo./15/1786, American Philosophical Society.

65 Wetherill, "Letter to Ministers."

66 Davis to Wetherill, 6 mo./24/1780, Wetherill Papers, FHL.

67 Matlack to Tenche Coxe, January 11, 1802 in Tenche Coxe Papers, HSP.

68 See Philadelphia Monthly Meeting Minutes: 5 mo./30/1783; Biddle's conflict of conviction was chronicled in the 1782 correspondence of James Pemberton and his brother, John. James, the clerk of Philadelphia Yearly Meeting and a member of the Philadelphia Monthly Meeting, writes that Biddle was "under a dispensation of close trial and conflict" as early as the spring of '82. By year's end the Quaker clerk writes that Biddle "appeared in meeting manifesting a broken humble state of mind." Throughout this conflict Pemberton expresses his admiration of Biddle and hopes that the "wayward Friend" will "find the waters of Jordan most effectual to his restoration" to the Society of Friends. (See Correspondance of James and John Pemberton for the year of 1782 in Pemberton Papers, HSP).

69 See Mekeel, Relation of Quakers, 217; and Mekeel, "Free Quakers of New England." Mekeel points out that there were distinct differences between the Pennsylvania Free Quakers and their New England bretheren. The Free Quakers of New England were more conservative, following the discipline of the Society on every issue with the exception of paying taxes to the Revolutionary government. Hence, they emerged as a group on a single issue and when that issue ceased to exist, they eventually disbanded. The Free Quakers of Pennsylvania, however, were composed of a much more complex constituency. Since they based their rule of conduct and action on freedom from the restraints of the Society of Friends, they welcomed all former Friends into their ranks who had been disowned by the Society for any reason at any time. By maintaining the freedom of conscience as inspired by the inner light, they maintained a wider degree of tolerance than either the Society of Friends or the New England Free Quakers.

70 Mekeel, Relation of Quakers, 289. Samuel Wetherill Jr., maintained that the Free Quakers had "no new doctrine to teach" but rather wished to be "freed from every species of eccleisiastical tyranny" of the Society of Friends. It was because of this wish that the group adopted the name "FreeQuakers."

Appendices

Appendix #1: *The following address was printed as a broadside on April 24, 1781. It was the first public address printed by the Free Quakers who, at this time, were a very small group. In order to explain their cause in forming a new religious organization, as well as to attract like-minded Friends, the Free Quakers distributed this broadside throughout the city of Philadelphia. (Quoted in Charles Wetherill's* History of the Free Quakers, *1894, pp. 47-49).*

An Address
To Those of the People called Quakers, who have been disowned for Matters Religious or Civil

Friends and Fellow Sufferers. -- The scattered and distressed situation in which we have been for some time past, having occasioned great inconvenience to most of us, a small number of men, educated among the people called Quakers, as you have been, have met together and seriously considered our circumstances.

This separation has not been sought by, but forced upon, us as the pride and folly of former churches, vainly attempting to abridge the rights of conscience, excommunicated their bretheren from among them. And there appears no reasonable ground of expectation that we shall ever again be united to those who have disowned us; for they will not permit among them that Christian liberty of sentiment and conduct which all are entitled to enjoy, and which we cannot consent to part with. You know that many have been disowned by that people for no other cause than a faithful discharge of those duties we owe to our country.

Thus situated, and acknowledging our dependence upon the Supreme Being, and the duty of public worship which we owe to him, we have lamented the loss of those advantages which arise from religious communion, and have feared still greater loss in this respect, to our children and families. And therefore, although we know that "weakness is ours," and that difficulties and dangers surround us on every hand, confiding in the gracious promise of the Great Shepherd of his people, that he would "be with" even "two or three," wheresoever they are met together in his name, we have agreed, that as Friends and bretheren, we will endeavor to support and maintain public meetings for religious worship.

We have no new doctrine to teach, nor any design of promoting schisms in religion. We wish only to be freed from every species of ecclesiastical tyranny, and mean to pay a due regard to the principles of our forefathers, and to their rules and regulations so far as they apply to our circumstances, and hope, thereby, to preserve decency and to secure equal liberty to all. We have no design to form creeds or confessions of faith, but humbly to confide in those sacred lessons of wisdom and benevolence, which have been left us by Christ and His apostles, contained in the holy scriptures; and appealing to that divine principle breathed by the breath of God into the hearts of all, to leave every man to think and judge for himself, according to the abilities received, and to answer for his faith and opinions to him, who "seeth the secrets of all hearts," the sole Judge and sovereign Lord of conscience.

And feeling for you, as fellow-sufferers, a sympathy and brotherly affection, we think it our duty thus to communicate to you what we have done and are about to do, that you may, if you choose, partake with us in the blessings we seek and hope to obtain. As bretheren indeed, united in affliction "let us (agreeably to the counsel given by the Apostle Paul) consider one another, to provoke unto love and to good works; not forsaking the assemblying of ourselves together, as the manner of some is, but exhorting one another. And so much the more as ye see the day approaching." Be encouraged, and let us meet together and ask bread from him in whose hand it is, with an humble hope, that he who giveth food "to the young ravens which cry" will provide also for us. And in this hope we salute you with unfeigned affection.

Signed in and on behalf of the meeting,

Samuel Wetherill, Jun., *Clerk*

Philadelphia, *24th of the 4th Month, 1781*

APPENDICES

Appendix #2: *The first matter to be addressed at the Free Quakers' meeting for business was the formulation of a Discipline. In order to obtain the assistance of all disowned Friends who might wish to join their Society, the Free Quakers issued the following broadside on the fourth day of the sixth month. The piece clearly states the Free Quaker justification for compliance in the Revolutionary movement. Note the emphasis on the inextricable nature of religion and civic affairs. (Quoted in Charles Wetherill's* History of the Free Quakers, *1894, pp. 50-52).*

The Monthly Meeting of Friends, called by some
THE FREE QUAKERS

(Distinguishing us from those of our Bretheren who have disowned us.)

Held at Philadelphia, The 4th Day of the 6th Month, 1781

TO OUR FRIENDS AND BRETHEREN IN PENNSYLVANIA, NEW JERSEY AND ELSEWHERE: --

Dear Friends. -- Agreeable to the intimations given you in our late "Address to those of the People called Quakers, who have been disowned for matters religious or civil," we have for some time past held two public meetings for worship on the first day of the week, and a meeting for the conducting of the business of the society, on the first second day of the week in each month. These meetings have afforded us great satisfaction, we shall continue them, with a firm hope that the blessing of heaven will, "as the dew of Hermon," descend in silence upon them.

In our deliberations on this subject we have been led to consider "That the Creator of man having bestowed upon individuals greater and less natural abilities and opportunities of

139

improvement, a variety of sentiments respecting the duties which we owe to him necessarily arises among us, and it becomes essential to our happiness that we may perform those duties in that way which we think the most acceptable to him. And therefore when we contemplate the long and earnest contest which has been maintained, and the torrents of blood which, in other countries, have been shed in defence of this precious privilege, we cannot but acknowledge it to be a signal instance of the immediate care of a divine providence over the people of America, that he has in the present great revolution, thus far established among us governments under which no man, who acknowledges the being of a God, can be abridged of any civil rights on account of his religious sentiments, while other nations, who see and lament their wretched situation, are yet groaning under a grievous bondage. But government established upon these liberal, just, and truly Christian principles, and wisely confined to the great objects of ascertaining and defending civil rights, in avoiding the possibility of wounding the conscience of any, must necessarily leave some cases unprovided for, which come properly under the care of religious societies. Hence we are not only left at liberty to act agreeably to our sentiments, but the necessity and obligation of establshing and supporting religious societies, are increased and strengthened.

We acknowledge the kindness of Providence in awakening us to a view of the deplorable situation in which we have been: disowned and rejected by those among whom we have been educated, and without a hope of being ever again united to them: separated and scattered abroad, as if we had been aliens in a strange land: the prospect of our situation has indeed humbled us: but that mercy which, "to an hair's breadth," covers the judgement seat of God, has preserved us, and induced us to confide that he will care for us. Being made sensible of the indispensable necessity of uniting together, we have cast our care upon God, and depending upon him for support, conceive it to be a duty which we owe to ourselves, our children, and families, to establish and support among us public meetings for religious worship, to appoint stated meetings for conducting the affairs of the Society, upon principles as liberal and enlarged toward one another, as those adopted by the State are toward all, and paying a due regard to the principles of our forefathers, and the spirit of the wise regulations established by them, to fix upon such rules as may enable us to preserve decency and good order: and among other things, to agree upon and make known a decent form of marriage, which may at once secure the rights of parents and children: and a mode of forming and preserving records of marriages, births, and burials.

For these purposes an essay of discipline, founded on that of our ancestors, has been formed, and laid before the meeting for business. A good degree of unanimity of sentiments thereupon has appeared among us; but we have thought it proper to leave it open for further consideration, and thus to communicate to our friends what we are about to do, in order to avail ourselves of the advice and assistance of all who may kindly afford us their counsel. And we sincerely and earnestly desire that we may obtain and be guided by that "wisdom from above," which is sufficient to overcome every danger and difficulty which we may have to contend against, and finally unite us together, in a truly Christian fellowship, and in the bonds of peace. Signed by order of the Meeting,

Samuel Wetherill, Jr., *Clerk.*

Appendix #3: *Since the Free Quakers of Philadelphia were in need of a suitable place in which to hold their meetings for worship and business, they appealed to the main body of Friends who had disowned them for permission to use one of the meetinghouses of that Society. They argued that the Society of Friends separated themselves from them, and that they, unwillingly, were forced to separate from the Society. Because of these circumstances their orthodox bretheren had no right to to exclude them from the joint use of the meetinghouses and burial grounds of Quakers. This argument was printed in the following address and delivered by Timothy Matlack to the Philadelphia Monthly Meeting. (Quoted in Charles Wetherill's* History of the Free Quakers, *1894, pp. 53-56).*

From the Monthly Meeting of Friends, called by some,

THE FREE QUAKERS,

Held by Adjournment at Philadelphia, on the 9th Day of the 7th Month, 1781.

TO THOSE OF OUR BRETHEREN WHO HAVE DISOWNED US: --

Bretheren. -- Among the very great number of persons whom you have disowned for matters religious and civil, a number have felt a necessity of uniting together for the discharge of those religious duties which we undoubtedly owe to God and to one another. We have accordingly met, and having seriously considered our situation, agreed to establish and endeavor to support, on the ancient and sure foundation, meetings for public worship, and meetings for conducting our religious affairs. And we rejoice in a firm hope, that as we humble ourselves before God, his presence will be found in them, and his blessing descend and rest upon them.

As you have by your proceedings against, separated yourselves from, us and declared that you have no unity with us, you have compelled us, however unwillingly, to become separate from you. And we are free to declare to you and the world, that we are not desirous of having any mistake which we happen to make laid to your charge; neither are we willing to have any of your errors brought as guilt against us. To avoid these, seeing that you have made the separation, we submit to have a plain line of distinction made between us and you. But there are some points which seem to require a comparison of sentiments between you and us, and some kind of decision to be made upon them. The property of that Society of which we and you were
once joint members, is far from being inconsiderable, and we have done nothing which can afford even a pretension of our having forfeited our right therein.

Whether you have or have not a right to declare to the world your sentiments of the conduct of any individual; or whether you have or have not a right to sit in judgement over and pass sentence upon your Christian bretheren differing in sentiment from you, although educated among you, are not questions now to be considered; but you have taken upon you to do those things, it remains only to be enquired, what are the consequences in law and equity of your having so done. Surely you will not pretend that our right is destroyed by those acts of yours. But we suggest to your consideration, whether your conduct has or has not disqualified you to hold any part of that property? A serious and full consideration, of this question, and the critical and strikingly singular situation in which you stand, cannot injure you; but it may, possibly, induce you to consider, with the more candour and readiness, what equity requires to be done by you toward us, or by us toward you; and tend to a decision the most proper between bretheren differing in sentiment one from another concerning their respective rights to property, yet each believing in him whose precept leads us, "to do unto others as we would they should do unto us."

Whatever may have been the consequences to yourselves, either of your conduct toward us as friends to the present revolution; or of your conduct in other cases, less immediately respecting us, it seems to be unquestionably certain, that we have not done anything which can possibly forfeit our right. And we see no reason why we should surrender it up to you; but think it a duty incumbent on us to assert our claim.

As a place for holding our meetings for worship and meetings for business relative to the Society, is become necessary for us, since you have separated yourselves from us, by testifying against us, and thereby rendering it highly improper for us to appear among you, as one people, at your meetings, we think it proper for us to use, apart from you, one of the houses built by Friends in this city for those purposes. We are desirous of doing this in the most decent and unexceptionable manner, and we are willing to hear anything which you may choose to say on the subject. And therefore we thus invite you to the opportunity of doing it, and of showing what degree of kindness and brotherly love toward us, still remains among you. We also mean to use the burial ground, whenever the occasion shall require it. For, however, the living may contend surely the dead may lie peaceably together.

Lest any may infer too much from this representation, we think it proper explicitly to declare, that should our right to the property in question be found, in the law, to be superior to yours, from any consideration whatever, it is far, very far from our wish to seclude you from a joint participation with us in the use of it. Neither do we mean to solicit a decision in law, unless you by your conduct compel us to it.

We sincerely and earnestly desire to have this subject amicably, equitably and speedily adjusted, and request that this free communication of our sentiments may be made known to all who are usually consulted on business among you, and that, for this purpose, it may be read when you next meet together on religious business.

As Christians, labouring in some degree to forgive injuries, we salute you, and though rejected by you, we are your friends and bretheren. Signed in and on behalf of the said Meeting by,

Samuel Wetherill, Jr., *Clerk.*

Appendix #4: *The following letter was written by the founder of Free Quakerism, Samuel Wetherill Jr., in 1793 and reflects his genuine commitment to the beliefs of that Society. The letter was provoked by the remarks of orthodox Friends from Philadelphia Yearly Meeting, who allegedly claimed that Wetherill should reconcile his differences with the Society of Friends during his remaining years on earth in order to prepare for the after life. (Quoted in Charles Wetherill's* History of the Free Quakers, *1894, pp. 97-110).*

Letter From Samuel Wetherill.

To The Second Day's Morning Meeting of Ministers and Elders, of the People Called Quakers in the City of Philadelphia: --

I have received a verbel message by Henry Drinker which I understand came from you: On this message I propose to make a few remarks. Such are the effects of long established forms in society, that I have no reason to expect I shall convince you of the impropriety of your message; yet I request you will read what I have to offer with as much candour as you can command on the occasion: I shall then be perfectly easy at whatever conclusions you may draw, or conduct you may observe towards me in the future part of your lives.

The message delivered to me was to the following purport, and as nearly verbatim as my memory serves me: Viz. "Thou must remember what is written 'When thou comest to offer thy gift if thou rememberest that thy Brother hath ought against thee, first go and be reconciled to thy Brother, and then come and offer thy gift:' Thy appearing as thou hast done has given pain to friends; we wish thee to be quiet in future; for a person appearing on such occasions, making the appearance of a friend, and one we have no unity with; is what friends, cannot dispense with, we therefore wish thee to be quiet in future; but if thou shouldst not, friends will be under the necessity of declaring publically, that thou art not in fellowship with them."

Before I reply to the foregoing, permit me a little to premise. The subject is serious. It is now many years since the Lord in a way not less than miraculous, visited my soul with his Love and Light, giving me to see a Beauty in a virtuous life far greater than anyone can comprehend who has not had the same Divine prospect; for altho' most men will admit the necessity of virtue, yet no man living sees fully into its beauty and infinite importance, until the Divine Light in an extraordinary manner opens it to him. This prospect ravished my soul, and begot in me so ardent a Love to the Lord, as that I then knew, and felt, what it was that supported the Martyrs in the flames; for I thought, if I had then an hundred lives, I could have sacrificed them all, if it had been required, for the Testimony of Jesus. At this time I entered into a covenant with my God, and made a total consecration of my heart to him. This was the day of my espousal to the beloved of Souls. This experience thus related is not meant to make a parade of superior virtue. I am far from feeling any vanity of this kind, I know my weaknesses and confess them, am poor, and have often stumbled in the way cast up for the redeemed to walk in; and have much reason to be concerned that so Divine a favour together with many others since have not produced a greater effect: But from the day of my first visitation until the present day, I have thought it my duty, by example and sometimes by precept, to recommend to Mankind those things on which their present and future felicity depends. That this has been done but in an imperfect manner is confessed.

I now proceed to remark upon your message as delivered by Henry Drinker, viz: That before I offered my gift I should first be reconciled to my Brother. It is not necessary for me to explain what I conceive to be the meaning of this text as delivered by our Lord. I expect you mean by it, that I should first be restored to my fellowship with you, before I attempted to persuade any person to be serious, and prepare for death, and that it is an exceeding great

147

offence if done upon a spot of ground in which you claim a propriety. Supposing myself, or any other person among the least of Mankind, on so serious an occasion as that of a fellow creature being suddenly summoned into the immediate presence of the great Judge of Heaven and Earth, should feel a fervent wish that all might be prepared when the summons should be sent to them. In such a case would it be absolutely necessary to suspend expressing this wish until the person was admitted into fellowship with you? If so, he then misses the opportunity and another may never happen. Men of all denominations are usually invited to attend the funeral of their fellow-citizens; Jews, Turks and Heathens might be present on such an occasion: Jews, Turks, and Heathens believe in a future existence and that the virtuous will be happy and the wicked miserable. Now suppose the mind of either such person to be deeply impressed on an occasion so serious, and that either Turk, Jew or Heathen should exhort every one present to be serious and endeavor to prepare for Death, I ask you my Bretheren what possible ground could there be in such case for offence? All who are invited to attend on those occasions are on an equality: Death is common to all men; every one is alike interested in the awful consequences, and therefore none can have exclusive privileges to give advice on those occasions.

When the Lord represents to the mind the absolute necessity of preparation for Death, all have an equal right in his fear to express their wish for their fellow creatures, or to exhort them to prepare for this awful change; and that any one person whatever, making a profession of Piety should be offended at it us strange. I expect you admit that it is every man's duty to wish well for his neighbor. And, if so, then every man has a right and ought to be at liberty to do good to his neighbor, either by his advice or in such way as he may think most proper, so that a real good be the object: to the Lord alone is he accountable for the way and the manner. This is not intended to vindicate an intrusion either upon you, or upon any other persons. For as every man has a right to give his advice on any important occasion, he being accountable to the Lord, so every other man has a right also either to receive or to reject as he pleases what is so offered, he or they being accountable only to the Lord: so that you as individuals or as a body, have a right to receive or reject, any advice which may be offered to you by any person whatever. But where there is a promiscuous multitude of all persuasions collected together on an occasion interesting to all, there your publickly opposing what might be offered, would render you highly to blame; for there are numbers not under the same prejudices with you, and what you would reject, might be suited to the conditions of others, and well received by them. You may say, as Henry Drinker said; we have a rule to the contrary. It may be so, but you ought not to have such a rule. It is an infringement upon the rights of all Men, and not only so, but you presumtuously infringe upon the prerogative of the Lord, you thereby attempt to circumscribe his grace, and limit his Divine Light upon the human soul. You may object again and say, If persons have a right to come into our Graveyards and give us advice, they have the same right to come into our Meeting Houses, and impose their advice upon us there. To this I reply, the cases are not similar.

That freedom which a person might use innocently, or what might be the duty of him to express whose mind was seriously impressed at a funeral to a promiscuous multitude, might yet be very improper if exercised when you were assembled in your places for worship. There is a Divine reason and fitness in things which the upright see into and which cannot be determined or prescribed by any literal rule. A Man, not of your society, would be either right or wrong in speaking among you, according as he was either especially qualified or not, and the strong prejudices which you have against other Societies, altho' it be your fault, it yet ought to make every person exceedingly cautious, and examine well his authority, if he supposed it his duty, in your places of Worship to give you advice; for all should take care if possible not to offend those who even labor under the most deep-rooted prejudices. Now altho' every Man who might apprehend it his duty to give you advice should be extremely careful not to offend you if possible, and it is granted that you have a right either to hear him, or to refuse to hear him, you being accountable only to the Lord for your exercising this right; yet my bretheren on this subject I will give you my opinion even tho' it will have no weight. It s safest to hear what any sober man may have to say on the all important subject of Piety and virtue: this will give you no pain in a dying hour; the opposing him might. You should not forget the error of Judgement the Apostles of our Lord were under; for altho' they were immediately commissioned by him to preach the Gospel, and to work miracles in his name, yet such was their weakness that they forbad others doing the same, because they followed not with them; but remember they were not justified for this, but reproved by their Master.

Friends should also remember the liberty which their forefathers took in going into the places of Worship of other Societies and speaking among them, and in their burying grounds down to the present day. To this you will say; It was their duty to do so; But it cannot be the duty of a person of another Society to come and Preach to friends. The vanity of this declaration is exceeding great. If it is improper for a person not of your Society to give an exhortation at a funeral among you, or in your place of Worship, upon what principle is it right in you to exhort at the funerals of others, and in the place of Worship of other Societies? Are you as a Society quite complete in all Christian Graces, and have you all divine qualifications bestowed upon you exclusively to the rest of men, so as that it is impossible to suppose the Lord could with any propriety authorize any other person beside a Quaker to speak to you? Can you show that you have an exclusive right to that divine illumination which expands the heart, and warms it with good will towards all men? Until you can show that every member among you is so perfect as that friendly advice bestowed upon them is altogether needless, or that qualification to give advice is possessed by you exclusively, your forbidding any person to give advice anywhere is improper. It is indeed, as has been observed, presuming to limit the Authority of the Highest, and is an attempt to prevent the Salvation of Men. But do not my friends suppose from this, that I have any inclination to visit you in this way. I hope that no such thing will ever happen; it would be the most painful task ever required of me, so unwilling am I to offend you, or to have any altercation with you.

Having remarked as above, it may not be improper to show you, that whilst you are faulting persons and proceeding against them in a high tone of unwarranted authority, for simply offering advice to such as are willing to receive it, without meaning an offence, or an obtrusion upon any; you are at the same time indecently intruding with your advice upon the clear and unquestionable rights of others. I could illustrate this by a variety of instances, but for brevity sake one shall suffice. I consider the Monthly Meeting and the select meeting of Philadelphia, as one body. Some friends by deputation from the monthly meeting waited upon two of my sons to deal with them for joining another religious Society. I was present at the conversation and the friends were treated with great decency and had a clear and full answer given them by my sons, that they chose to go to the same place of worship with their father: A visit was notwithstanding afterwards repeated, at which I happened accidently to be present, and as it was in my own House, and the business with my own children in whose welfare I am deeply interested, so I thought, I might without any impropriety say something on the occasion and more especially on such an occasion. What was said, was very civilly said. I was however replied to precisely to the following effect: That friends' business was with my children, and not with me, that I had no business there, and must have come to interupt friends in their visit. That my children were of age and should judge for themselves, that their father was a prejudiced person and his advice not to be regarded.

If it be an intrusion of an aggravated kind for a person not of your Society to walk into your burying ground to attend a funeral and there to express a wish that all might be serious and prepare to die, how much greater is that intrusion you are guilty of, when after you had been decently received in my house, and a clear and full answer given you to your advice, you still repeat it and claim a right, and exercise it too, to give your advice again and again, and tell myself I had no business there, that my children should take your advice, and not their Father's, for his they ought not to regard. Let me ask you my friends -- How would you treat men who should act in the same way towards you, and your children? You would I doubt not, expatiate upon such intrusion, and would treat such persons with contempt. If there has been an impropriety in me in obtruding advice (which will be impossible for you to prove) yet when compared with yours it is small, and what our Lord said to a people formerly, who was apt to find fault is applicable to you. "Why beholdest thou the mote that is in my brother's eye, and seest not the beam which is in thine own: first take the beam out of thine own eye and then shalt thou see clearly how to take out the mote which is in thy Brother's eye."

Having made the foregoing observations on the rights of Men, it remains to say a few words respecting another part of your message. The writer of this has not an high opinion of his gifts or abilities to promote the cause of virtue, he can say however he wishes well to it sincerely, and in his feeble engagements therein, sometimes feels a peace Men can neither give nor take away. But yet he will confess to you, altho' you have no authority to call him to an account, nor interfere in his business, he at times feels some pain least he should not have advanced so great and good a cause. But friends, have there not been appearances among you which have given you pain when the fault lay with yourselves? I was a diligent attender of your meetings for near thirty years, and knew that a part of your meeting were uneasy at the public appearances of some whose Ministry they at length approved. I well remember George Dillwyn's first appearance in the Ministry, and the opposition he met with. There was at that time a particular intimacy between that friend and myself, and as bretheren we freely unbosomed our hearts to each other. After repeated opposition to him both in public and private from members of your meeting, a committee told him plainly that they had not unity with his appearance; And they enjoined him not to break silence but to bear his burden, and more especially not to appear in Prayer, for if he did, they told him they would manifest their Testimony against him publically by not joining with him, and in order still the more effectually to stop his mouth, one public friend who is not now among the living, but who was in his day of distinguished note among you, wrote a letter to George, and in clear and express words told him, that he had neither part nor lot in the ministry, or, says the friend, "the Lord never spoke by me." As I knew the opposition to George arose from prejudice, and having a great love for him, I related to my Father-in-law what was carrying on against George, upon which my father appeared much surprised and altho' he was a member of your meeting, did not seem aware of what was doing; which shows there may not always be unanimity among yourselves on business of this kind: for my Father immediately interested himself in George's favour and spoke to John Smith at Burlington (George having then removed there) and requested John to use his influence in George's favour, and I well knew that Mordecai Yarnal, Anthony Benezet and John Smith together with some other friends, whose names I could not mention who were then members of your meeting, most of whom are since dead, so interposed in George's behalf that at length he was admitted a minister among you.

Upon the whole then, If the most eminent ministers among you at times give you pain, and you do with so much determination oppose members of your own Society, meerly upon ill founded prejudices, what must such poor creatures expect, who have been declared by you not worthy of Christian fellowship. Is it possible after such a declaration, that you can possess that simplicity and candour towards them in which alone there is true discernment? Further I was informed that if I should again appear as I had done, friends would be under the necessity of informing such who might be present that I was not in unity with friends.

If you entertain an Idea that I wish to avail myself of any reputation which might result from a supposed membership with you, you are under a great mistake. It has happened divers times since I have been disowned, that I have fallen in company with persons who had an esteem for friends, and have found some respect paid me upon a supposition that I belonged to the Society.

153

Now it ever appeared to me a kind of hypocrisy if I should let a person go away under such a mistake, and enjoy that sort of reputation which I was not entitled to, and have always undeceived them, frankly telling them I was disowned by you: so that if such a case should happen as you allude to, you have not only a right to do as you say, but you have my entire approbation so to do; however in this explanation of yourselves, you ought to take care not to defame me, there might be some persons present on such an occasion, who might not be acquainted with the merits of the case for which I was disowned; such might suppose I was disowned by you for some great immorality: be pleased therefore to state the whole case, and I have neither right nor inclination to prevent it, for I have scarcely ever met with one person, either a member of your Society, or of any other, who did not think I was hardly dealt with by you, and by far the greater number consider you as the aggressor. A man may be disowned by you, and held up as a spectacle of contempt, who nevertheless may be owned by Christ at the day of general judgement, and admitted into fellowship with the Saints. But let us now enquire into the nature of that offence which was esteemed of such magnitude as to render it necessary to testify against me. It was simply for submitting to the dispensations of Divine Providence, which you yourselves have since done, for this no offence, have I been, and am still to be, held up by you in an odious light, and pains taken to stamp a prejudice against me upon the minds of the rising generation, so that when both you and I are dead and all of us in that most awfull state of existence, future generations may treat my memory as you have done my person.

The amazing prejudices you labour under, and your conduct governed by those prejudices, operate as an injury for ages: And yet my friends you changed your sentiments with respect to the offence for which you disowned me, for you desisted from the business you begun, and many continued members of your meeting who yet acted as myself had done; And Anthony Benezet freely acknowledged to me you were wrong. The candour of this worthy Man in making this voluntary confession to one who before he had blamed, very much endeared him to me, it was a concession I neither expected nor sought for: But you, my friends not possessing his virtues, still persecute the Man whom you at first injured.

There are divers members of your meeting for whom I have always entertained an high esteem. I have taken them to be Persons of more enlarged and liberal minds than to act towards me as you do, were they not under the necessity of joining with you for form sake. If there are such among you, they are excepted in the censure comprehended in this address. But I may be mistaken, you may be unanimous, and it is possible your conduct may not be so much the effect of ill will towards me, as an error in your judgement, you have been accustomed to certain rules, perhaps long established, which you conceive indispensably necessary to observe; how far this will excuse you at the day that is hastening is not for me to say; but this dry, formal, undistinguishing sort of business, leads at times to the same conduct as that of the Scribes and Pharisees, who bid the Apostles be silent, and excommunicated Men for believing in Christ.

Altho' the writer of this is of little consequence in your esteem, nor of much in his own, he is yet serious in this address and thinks it is not inconsistent with a becoming degree of modesty to request you would read it with solid attention in your meeting; tho' this he does not expect. But were you to do so, divested of prejudice, you might derive from it some instruction which would be of future service to you, both in your individual capacities, and as members of a Religious Society.

The foregoing was written just before the breaking out of the malignant fever, and was intended to have been sent to you then, but the writer's attention was taken off from this, on account of the extreme attention to his business which he was hurried into, occasioned by the afforesaid disease, and the great mortality which happened in consequence. The particulars of that exhortation which gave you offence, and occasioned your message to him. The writer does not pretend to the knowledge of future events, except those which must happen in the nature of things; but Divine providence may make use of an instrument to give warning to prepare for those things which he may intend to bring about, without revealing to such instrument his particular designs. The writer well remembers his mind was seriously impressed with the extreme shortness of our existence here; and of the uncertainty of all things below; and of the infinite importance of a preparation for death; this prospect so impressed his mind that he thought they were as powerful reasons for deep consideration and preparation for death, as if the Lord should again at that instant commission an Angel to declare, in the Awfull manner one formerly did to John the Divine that time should be no longer. This prospect the writer thought it his duty to express, and which he did as well as he was then abilitated to do. And, my friends, let me ask you what authority have you to reprove him for it? Has not the great mortality with which the City has been visited, shown the propriety of such an exhortation from some person? And how came you by a right to dictate either who should or who should not be the instrument to urge those things. What was then offered did not offend all who were present, I have been assured, but on the contrary was well received; and the late visitation esteemed a corroborating circumstance to show its propriety. Many who were then present are now no more in mutability, and among this number is one, or more, of your Meeting, and if the Ancient friend who probably reported to you what happened, and no doubt agreed to the measure adopted by you, had taken the advice then given, instead of spurning at it, and so improved the few moments allotted to him in the evening of his day, as was then sincerely urged, it would have been acting a wiser part; and altho' we may hope he is at rest, together with other members of your meeting, who agreed in your message to the subscriber, yet their officiousness in this business is now no cause or part of their felicity, nor will it contribute to yours, my bretheren, in the day that is hastening. Your conduct towards the subscriber, will not be among the good works in which the righteous rejoice.

Such is the esteem which the writer has entertained for divers members of your meeting, and so great has been his desire to live upon the most friendly terms with them, that he is sorry he is obliged to write as he has done; he wishes sincerely to cultivate the most cordial friendship for his fellow Christians of all denominations; he therefore hopes there are divers members of your meeting to whom the censure contained in this address is not applicable, it would give him pain to think otherwise, because he wishes still to love and esteem them. But if your meeting is unanimous and those persons so loved and esteemed look upon the subscriber in that point of view which the meeting's conduct towards him fully implies, he will endeavor to bear with their prejudices and patiently wait the event of all things here below, hoping and believing his weak efforts to promote the cause of virtue, will through his Master's clemency finally receive his approbation. And being supported in this faith and confidence he hopes when Jesus commissions, he shall undismayed at all fit times and places warn Men to prepare for an Awfull Eternity. Your advice and threats are therefore my friends, considered in the same light, as if you forbid the writer, to Love his Lord and Saviour.

Samuel Wetherill.

Philadelphia, 11 mo. 23rd, 1793.

Appendix #5: *On the Sixth day of the Eighth month, 1781 at their Meeting for Business, the Free Quakers unanimously agreed to a Discipline. The document was filled with a spirit of patriotism as well as one of Christian devotion and reflects the mission of the Society as its members envisioned their role in the Early Republic. (Quoted from Charles Wetherill's* History of the Free Quakers, *1894, pp. 26-32).*

The Discipline

of the

Society of Friends, by some styled the Free Quakers

The Creator of man, having bestowed upon individuals greater and less natural abilities, and opportunities of improvement, a variety of sentiments respecting the duties which we owe to him, necessarily arises among us, and it becomes essential to our happiness, that we may perform those duties in that way which we think most acceptable to him. And therefore, when we contemplate the long continued and earnest contest which has been maintained, and the torrents of blood which, in other countries, have been shed in defence of this precious privilege, we cannot but acknowledge it to be a signal instance of the immediate care of a divine providence over the people of America, that he has, in the present great revolution, thus far established among us governments, under which no man, who acknowledges the being of a God, can be abridged of any civil right on account of his religious sentiments; while other nations who see and lament their wretched situation are yet groaning under a grievous bondage. But governments established upon those liberal, just, and truly Christian principles, and wisely confined to the great objects of ascertaining and defending civil rights, in avoiding the possibility of wounding the conscience of any, must unavoidably leave some cases unprovided for, which come properly under the care of religious societies. Hence we are not only left at liberty to act agreeably to our sentiments; but the necessity and obligation of establishing and supporting religious societies are increased and strengthened.

We acknowledge the kindness of providence in awakening us to a view of the deplorable situation in which we have been. Disowned and rejected by those among whom we have been educated, and scattered abroad, as if we had been aliens in a strange land, the prospect of our situation has indeed humbled us. But he whose mercy endureth forever has preserved us, and induced us to confide that he will care for us. And being made sensible of the indispensable necessity of uniting together, we have cast our care upon the great preserver of men, and depending upon him for our support, conceive it to be a duty which we owe to ourselves, our children and families, to establish and support among us public meetings for religious worship; to appoint stated meetings for conducting the affairs of the Society, upon principles as liberal and enlarged toward one another, as those adopted by the state are toward all, and paying a due regard to the principles of our forefathers, and the spirit of the wise regulations established by them, to fix upon such rules as may enable us to preserve decency and good order; and among other things, to agree upon, and make known a decent form of marriage, which may at once secure the rights of parents and of children; and a mode of forming and preserving records of marriages, births and burials.

Wherefore after mature deliberation it was unanimously agreed as follows, to wit: --

First. -- Meetings for public worship shall be established and kept up. The time and place of holding them shall be ordered and directed by the meeting for business. And it is earnestly recommended, to all who come to our meetings for worship, or meetings for business, to attend precisely at the time appointed.

Secondly. -- A meeting shall be held monthly for the conducting of the business of the Society, in which any member may freely express his sentiments, on all business which shall there be determined or considered. In this meeting unanimity and harmony ought to prevail, and where any difference of sentiment may appear, charity and brotherly condescesion ought to be shown to one another. Minutes of all proceedings shall be kept, and for this purpose a clerk shall be appointed, and be under the direction of the meeting. At the opening of each meeting, after a solemn pause for worship, the minutes of the meeting next preceeding shall be read.

Thirdly. -- Persons intending marraige may, either in person or by friend, inform the meeting for business thereof; but where it may conveniently be, it is recommended, that the parties proposing marriage do attend the meeting before which the proposal is made. Whereupon a committee shall be appointed to enquire concerning their clearness of other marriage engagements, consent of parents or guardians; and such other matters as relate to the proposed marriage, and report thereon to the next meeting. No reasonable objection appearing, and the parties as aforesaid signifying the continuation of their intentions, the marriage may be allowed of, and two persons appointed to attend the decent solemnization thereof, and to have the certificate of the same recorded in the book of marriages.

The marriage may be solemnized at a public meeting for worship; or at the house of either of the parties; or at the house of their parents or friends, as the parties may choose,: but it is recommended that the same be preceded by a solemn pause, and worship to God. As cases may probably happen, in which it may be inconvenient to postpone marriages so long as from one monthly meeting to another, in such cases an adjournment of the meeting may be made, the report of the committee received, and the marriage be allowed of as aforesaid.

The solemnization is recommended to be after the following manner to wit: The parties standing up and taking each other by the hand, the man shall declare to this import: That he takes the woman, naming her name, to be his wife, and will be unto her a loving and faithful husband until death shall separate them. And the woman, on her part, shall declare to the import that she takes the man, naming his name, to be her husband: and will be unto him a loving and faithful wife until death separate them. The certificate whereof may be of the following import, to wit: Whereas A. B, of C., (expressing also his title or occupation,) son of C. D., of E. and F. his wife, and G. H., daughter of I. K., of L., and M., his wife, having laid their intentions of marriage with each other, before the meeting for business of the Society of Friends, styled by some the Free Quakers, held at N., the same were allowed of, and on the day of the   month, in the year of our Lord (inserting the day, month and year), the said parties appeared at a meeting appointed for the solemnization of the said marriage (or otherwise as the case may be), and taking each other by the hand, the said A.B., did, in a solemn manner, declare that he took the said G. H., to be his wife, and promised to be unto her a loving and faithful husband until death should separate them: And the said G. H., did in like manner declare, that she took the said A. B., to be her husband, and promised to be unto him a loving and faithful wife until death should separate them. And in confirmation and testimony of the same, they the said A. B. and G. H., she assuming the name of her husband, did then and there to these presents set their hands. And we, whose names are also subscribed, being present at the said marriage and subscription, have, as witnesses to the same, hereunto set our hands, the day and year aforesaid.

Fourthly. -- Records shall be kept of all marriages, birth, and burials among us. And as these records may be of great importance, and the recording of births and burials will greatly depend on the care of individuals, in giving an account thereof, it is earnestly recommended to all, to give an early account of both, mentioning the child's name, parentage, and day of its birth; and the name, parentage, title or occupation, age and day of decease, as well of those who die abroad, when the same can be ascertained, as of those who die among us.

Fifthly. -- Persons desirous of joining us in Society, signifying the same to the meeting of business, and appearing to be of good character, may be admitted. Whereupon they may give in the names and ages of their children, to be recorded. Shall any choose to go from among us, a minute thereof may be entered among our proceedings.

Sixthly. -- In cases of controversy respecting property, a reference to disinterested men, either of our own or some other Society, and a compliance with their judgment, may be recommended, as the most expeditious and least expensive mode of terminating such disputes, and tending to peace and harmony, but, it shall be a perpetual rule among us, as a religious society, that we will not otherwise interfere in controversies between one man and another. This rule being contrary to that of our ancestors, in this case we think it necessary to observe, That however blameable or even "shameful" it might have been in the Apostle's day, for brother to go to law with brother "before the unbelievers" in the present day, when the State, of which we ourselves are members, appoint men eminent for their abilities and integrity, to judge of all controversies, and those judges being themselves Christians, are aided by juries of Christians: there does not appear any just cause for prohibiting appeals to them: on the contrary, to us it seems to be indecent and unjust to speak of these Christian courts, as the Apostles spake of those of "the unbelievers," and as the Society who have disowned us have affected to speak of the courts of justice, even when themselves were the officers, jurors, judges, and legislators.

Seventh. -- As brethren each may counsel and advise another in the spirit of meekness, as he may see other in the spirit of love and meekness, as he may see occasion, remembering always that he also may be tempted: but leaving guilt to be punished by the laws of the land, and commending those who err to the grace of God, no public censures shall be passed by us on any. Neither shall a member be deprived of his right among us, on account of his differing in sentiment from any or all of his brethren, he being accountable only to the Lord.

Appendix #6: *List of members who belonged to the Free Quaker Society in the eighteenth century (Taken from Charles Witherill's* History of the Free Quakers, *1894, pp. 111-114)*

Nathaniel Allen
Matthew Ash
Jonathan Ash
Peter Barker
Moses Bartam, Trustee
John Bartram
James Bartram
John Bell
Enoch Betts
Clement Biddle
Owen Biddle
Margaret Bodds
Joseph Bonsall
Joshua Bonsall
Jonathan Bonsall
James Boone
Nathaniel Brown,
    Trustee
Thomas Bryan
Abner Buckman
John Buckman, Jr.
Joseph Burden
Hannah Carmalt
George Chandler
John Chapman
John Claypoole
Elizabeth Claypoole
    (aka Betsy Ross)
Thomas Coats
Martha Coats
Sarah Coats
Isaac Collins (of
    Trenton)
Samuel Crawford
Elizabeth Crawford
Mary Crawford
Charles Crawford
Elizabeth Crawford, Jr.
Sarah Cribs

Mary Cribs
Samuel Crispin
William Crispin
Thomas Crispin
Lydia Crispin
Lydia Crispin, Jr.
Samuel Crispin, Jr.
William Darragh
Lydia Darragh
Ann Darragh
Sussanna Darragh
Timothy Davis
James Delaplaine
Cadwalder Dickinson
Johnathan Draper
Thomas Dyer
Jehu Eldridge
Samuel Eldridge
Nathaniel Elliot
Thomas Elton
John Elton
Elizabeth Elton
Anthony Elton
Sussanna Elton
Mary Elton
Thomas Elton, Jr.
Sussanna Elton, Jr.
Joshua Ely
Edward Evans
Evan Evans
David Evans
J. Fisher
William Fisher, Jr.
Samuel Foulke
Nathaniel Gibson
Joseph Govett
Edward Griffiths
Rebecca Gumbes
Edward Heston

Caleb Hewes
Henry Hewes
Thomas Hopkins
Samuel Howell
Isaac Howell, Trustee
Robert Jones
Jacob Karcher
Elinor Karcher
Margaretta Karcher
John Knight
Jacob Lahn
Thomas Lang
Margaret Lang
Agnes Lang
James Lang
Margaret Lang, Jr.
Mary Lawn
Richard Leedom
Eli Lewis
Anne Lewton
Joshua Lippincott
Sarah Lippincott
Christopher Marshall,
    Trustee
Timothy Matlack
William Matlack
White Matlack, Treasurer
William Milnor
John Morris
Samuel Morris
Elizabeth Murphy
Aaron Musgrave
J. Musgrave
Elizabeth Neave
Elizabeth Neave, Jr.
Joseph Ogden
Joseph Ogden, Jr.
John Parrish
Robert Parrish

APPENDICES

165

Index

167

William C. Kashatus III is a teacher of history in the Philadelphia-area Independent School System and a Ph.D. candidate at the University of Pennsylvania. He graduated Phi Beta Kappa from Earlham College and holds a masters degree in history from Brown University. A summer seasonal ranger with the National Park Service at Independence National Historical Park, Kashatus' research interests include the American Revolution, Quaker influence in the shaping of colonial society and biographies of Early American personalities. His articles have appeared in several historical journals including Quaker History, Pennsylvania Heritage, The Virginia Social Science Journal and The Valley Forge Journal.